PART 4 PUNCTUATION AND MECHANICS

PART 5 THE RESEARCH-BASED ESSAY

A
BASIC
HANDBOOK
OF
WRITING
SKILLS

Pam Besser

JEFFERSON COMMUNITY COLLEGE

Mayfield Publishing Company
Mountain View, California
London • Toronto

Library of Congress Cataloging-in-Publication Data

Besser, Pam.
    A basic handbook of writing skills / Pam Besser.
        p.   cm.
    Includes index.
    ISBN 1-55934-032-0
    1. English language — Rhetoric — Handbooks, manuals, etc.
    2. English language — Grammar — Handbooks, manuals, etc.   I. Title.
    PE1408.B486   1993
    808'.042 — dc20   93-30095
                                                                                            CIP

Manufactured in the United States of America
10 9 8 7 6 5 4 3 2 1

Mayfield Publishing Company
1280 Villa Street
Mountain View, California 94041

Sponsoring editor, Janet M. Beatty; production editor, Sondra Glider; developmental editor, Leslie Taggart; manuscript editor, Carol Beal; text and cover designer, Terri Wright; manufacturing manager, Martha Branch; cover background, W. Cody/West Light. The text was set in 10½/12 Plantin Regular by Thompson Type and printed on 50# Arcata Opaque by Arcata Graphics.

Text credits appear on a continuation of the copyright page, p. 314.

For Rita, Tom, Tony, Alicia, Tighe, Lisa, Katie, and Maggie
Castigat Ridendo Mores and *Veritas Vos Liberabit*

PREFACE

The range of writing students' backgrounds and skills is wider than it's ever been. In teaching basic writing, I've coaxed the most effective communication from the widest range of beginning writers by presenting writing as a multidimensional process that includes prewriting, writing, and rewriting. Research studies indicate that grammar exercises are limited in their usefulness; students who become proficient at working through them do not necessarily become better writers. In fact, they often are unable to make the connection between their responses to programmed exercises and their own writing. What serves student writers best, in my experience, is a coupling of rhetorical instruction that explains and illustrates the writing process in friendly, accessible language with a grammatical reference that clarifies the conventions of Standard American English. This handbook offers this pairing in its concise coverage of the basics of writing.

The book starts where *all* writers must begin: by generating ideas, focusing their topic, and knowing the purpose of their writing. Part 1 continues with drafting, outlining, revising, and proofreading and editing the draft; within these four chapters are several drafts of complete student essays. Part 2 explains paragraph and sentence structures and includes examples of specific paragraph organizations, types of sentences, and common sentence errors. Part 3 examines sentence parts and correct word usage; it also offers instruction on using the dictionary and a separate chapter of alphabetized words that illustrate orthographic or semantic problems common to basic writers. Part 4 addresses punctuation and mechanics and includes examples of common errors and suggested corrections. Part 5 explains the research process and includes sample note cards, bibliography cards, and a complete student essay with MLA documentation.

Three features make this book a particularly practical and useful tool:

- *Format.* The plastic comb binding lets *A Basic Handbook of Writing Skills* lie flat, which makes it easy to use while working at a computer, typewriter, and anywhere that work space is at a premium. The page layout accentuates the clarity of the text presentation, making information easily accessible.
- *Emphasis on collaborative learning.* At the end of each chapter is a pairing of elements called "A Student Writes" and "A Classmate Responds" that offers student writing samples and practical advice on peer review. Included is the assignment and its purpose, the student's paragraph or essay draft, questions for peer review, a classmate's responses to those questions, and the student's revision of the draft. Not only do these elements illustrate to students the development and use of the specific skills presented in each chapter, but they also serve to bring students back to the reason for revising and editing — to communicate information to a reader.
- *Abundant guides to help readers find information.* Students unfamiliar with handbooks often have a difficult time navigating through them. In addition to the standard directories (the table of contents, index, page tabs, and chapter headers), other helpful references appear throughout the book. Inside the front cover is "A Quick Reference Guide," which lists chapter titles as well as questions students commonly ask about writing along with their appropriate page references. Each of the five parts opens with an outline of the chapters therein, complete with page references to chapter sections. Inside the back cover is a list of commonly used correction symbols with references to the corresponding chapters and sections within.

A separate Instructor's Manual provides numerous exercises that can be used in conjunction with the handbook. Also included are a suggested syllabus, teaching suggestions that include ideas for collaborative learning, and diagnostic tests.

Acknowledgments

This book is the result of my insistence that a handbook *can* be accessible to students regardless of their skills as writers. I am thankful that the people at Mayfield were in agreement with me from the very beginning. Thanks go to Sheila Kearney who insisted that I submit the manuscript to Mayfield for consideration. I appreciate the continued support of Jan Beatty, Senior Editor, whose belief in this project and whose insights helped me through the initial stages of the project. Accolades go to Leslie Taggart, developmental editor, whose wisdom, honesty, instinct, patience, good humor, and friendship motivated me and sustained me throughout the numerous drafts. Her suggestions and refinements permeate the text. The copyeditor, Carol Beal, and the production editor, Sondra Glider, and other members of the production team were wonderfully helpful and eager to teach me about the production process.

I wish to thank the following reviewers for their perceptive comments and suggestions:

Valerie Anthony, University of North Florida
David R. Dedo, Samford University
Mary Dunn, College of Lake County
Ann George, Pennsylvania State University
W. Gary Griswold, California State University,
    Long Beach
Sandra Hastings, Seattle Central Community College
Katherine Heenan, University of Connecticut
Dona J. Hickey, University of Richmond
Dennis P. Kriewald, Laredo Junior College
Judith Stanford, Rivier College
Jennifer Thompson, University of Kansas
Holly Zaitchik, Boston University

I also want to thank my students for their eagerness to learn from me, my colleagues for their willingness to share with me, and my family and friends for their patience to listen to me and their courage to support me. I have paid the piper and have been granted the pleasure of his music.

CONTENTS

PART 3: SENTENCE PARTS   127

Chapter 8: *Identifying Sentence Parts*   129

Chapter 18: *Italics (Underlining)*   235

Chapter 19: *Numbers and Abbreviations*   239

Chapter 20: *Capitalization*   245

PART 5: THE RESEARCH-BASED ESSAY   251

Chapter 21: *Gathering Information*   253

A
BASIC
HANDBOOK
OF
WRITING
SKILLS

Part 1

The Writing Process

Part 1   The Writing Process

Chapter 1

Generating Ideas

In the writing process there are three *stages* that you go through: inventing or planning, writing, and rewriting.

Inventing includes thinking about the topic, coming up with ideas, taking notes on first impressions, and jotting down and organizing your initial ideas.

Writing includes writing drafts and organizing information into a specific structure.

Rewriting includes revising (rethinking, reseeing, reorganizing) what you have written, proofreading (looking for errors), and editing (correcting errors).

Don't let the term *stages* make you feel boxed in — they don't happen 1–2–3. In fact, they double back on and overlap each other.

Let's say you are assigned a piece of writing on animal rights, but you know very little about animal rights. What do you do? You worry; you think again and again about the topic until you decide on a plan of action to gather information you will need before you write. The plan might include reading something about animal rights or asking questions of people who are knowledgeable about the topic. This is the inventing stage.

In the inventing stage you may often jot down ideas or a group of related ideas. You have then entered the writing stage, even if you are still coming up with ideas. You may even find yourself in the rewriting stage if, while you are writing, you decide to cross something out or make other changes. So you can be in all three stages at the same time — just as while you are shopping for dinner items, for example, you may think about what you plan to eat and then change your mind.

1a   Inventing and Planning

1a

What will you write about? Sometimes, instructors will give students a specific topic for writing; other times, students have a choice of topics. If you have a choice of topics, try to pick one you are comfortable with or already know something about. Either way, you need some tools for generating information about the topic.

1a-1 Long-Term Memory vs. Short-Term Memory

People have two types of memory: long-term memory and short-term memory. Long-term memory retains information you use daily — your name, your address, your background, who you are, who you know, and everything you have ever learned.

Short-term memory, however, is quite different. What happens when you are sitting in class and the instructor is talking rapidly? You try to take notes, and you get the first part and the last part of what the instructor says, but you forget all the information in the middle because you are trying to write down everything word for word. Your short-term memory will hold only a limited amount of information. You lose the rest of it, unless you can link it into your long-term memory. Thus, the best way to take notes in class is simply to sit and listen, comprehend the main ideas, and then jot down your own rewording of the ideas as notes.

The same is true with writing. Write down your ideas any way they come into your mind. You can always organize them later. It's better to go ahead and jot down all your ideas; then you can go back to them later to see if they will be useful. That way you won't forget them. In fact, writing down all your first ideas will actually help you find other ideas you might not have had otherwise.

Don't worry about the order of your ideas. Sometimes, the ending comes first; other times, the middle comes first. Or you may think, "I know what I want to say, but I don't know how to start." The following techniques will help you get started.

1a-2 Brainstorming

Brainstorming is writing down every single idea you have about a topic in the order that the ideas come into your mind. When you brainstorm, you don't worry about whether an idea seems ridiculous or stupid—you write down every idea even if you don't understand its connection to your other ideas. Writing your ideas in list form is one type of brainstorming.

Let's assume you are given a topic like advertising, which is very broad. What are you going to write about? Are you going to write about a certain category of ads, like car ads, cigarette ads, or perfume ads? Are you going to write about one particular car, cigarette, or perfume ad? Or are you going to write about how ads cause people to buy products? Do some brainstorming to help you decide what aspect of advertising you will write about. Write down every idea as it occurs to you, regardless of how irrelevant some of the ideas may seem. Write down as many ideas as you can. To illustrate the process, the following example gives a brainstorming list for advertising.

EXAMPLE 1: BRAINSTORMING ABOUT ADS

located everywhere	a lot of blue eyes
newspapers	power
magazines	wealth
television	immortality
billboards	friendship
grocery carts	liquor ads
use beautiful people	cigarette ads
music	perfume ads
short	sexy people
colorful	people having
not truthful	fun
don't say what's wrong with	great outdoors
the product	family situations
thin people in diet ads	feel good
gorgeous people in	no pain
makeup ads	

Once you have done some brainstorming, you can organize the information into lists by combining similar ideas. For example, the previous brainstorming list includes the following types of items: kinds of ads, contents of ads, effects of ads, places

1a

people can find ads, and promises ads make. These seem to be logical categories based on the similarities of some of the items listed. The following example illustrates the listed items categorized.

EXAMPLE 2: IDEAS ORGANIZED INTO LISTS

Kinds of Ads

liquor ads
cigarette ads
perfume ads

Contents of Ads

beautiful people
thin people in diet ads
gorgeous people in makeup ads
a lot of blue eyes
sexy people
people having fun
great outdoors
family situations

Effects of Ads

not truthful
don't say what's wrong with the product

Places Ads Are Located

located everywhere
newspapers
magazines
television
billboards
grocery carts

Promises Ads Make

power
wealth
immortality
friendship
feel good
no pain

Sometimes, items (like those that follow) do not fit into any of the categories. These items can probably be eliminated.

music
short
colorful

Brainstorming a list of ideas and then organizing the ideas according to general topics is a productive way to begin a writing task. Some of the lists in example 2, for instance, can be developed into a paragraph (or more) of explanation about a general area of advertising.

1a-3 Grouping Ideas

One way to start a draft on a topic is to **group the ideas,** as we did with the brainstorming list, and put them into a paragraph. Decide which group to use as a basis for writing a paragraph by looking at the types of items as well as the number of items in a particular list. Then, look at how those items relate to the topic. Do the items clarify or explain a main idea about the topic? Do the items illustrate something about the topic? The following example is a first draft of a paragraph using the items from the list "Places Ads Are Located."

EXAMPLE 1

Everywhere I go, I see ads that seem to jump out at me saying "buy this" or "buy that." When I look at newspapers, I notice ads for furniture stores, clothing stores, and grocery stores. Also, when I read my favorite magazines, I see ads for everything from running shoes to compact discs. Recently, while driving to school, I have noticed billboards screaming their messages, which I don't remember seeing before. In fact, I can't even go to the grocery without seeing ads stuck on the ends of carts.

The next example is a first draft of a paragraph that uses some of the items from the list "Contents of Ads."

EXAMPLE 2

Most ads show pictures of people who are too beautiful to be real, and they suggest that people who use their products will become just as beautiful. For example, makeup ads have pictures of gorgeous women who are very sexy. The advertisers want people to think that their makeup turns average-looking women into women who look like the models in the ads. In addition, diet ads always show thin people who look like they are having a great time eating diet products. Not only are all of these models beautiful and thin, but they also have blue eyes. Obviously, advertisers want people to believe that purchasing certain products will ensure beauty, thinness, and blue eyes.

Notice that some of the items in the list (great outdoors, family situations) were not used in this paragraph. These items can be either omitted or used to develop one or two separate paragraphs, depending on the purpose for writing.

1a-4   Freewriting

Many writers make the mistake of trying to write perfectly the first time. **Freewriting,** another way to find ideas, can help you learn to overcome this problem. Freewriting means writing down everything that comes to your mind for a certain amount of time—perhaps 5, 10, or 15 minutes—without correcting or censoring it. Don't lift your pen from your paper for whatever length of time you have decided to freewrite. Just keep writing. Get your ideas down as fast as you can and in any order. No one is going to see this particular piece of writing but you.

Sometimes, while you are writing, the right word won't come to mind, and you may lose the last part of your thought. To avoid losing those thoughts, write the first part of the sentence, leave a line blank whenever you find yourself pausing to search for a word, and then finish your thought. When you go back and reread what you've written, usually the missing word will come to your mind, and you can fill in the blank. The following examples show how this technique works.

FREEWRITING EXAMPLE 1

What about advertising? TV ads or magazine ads? TV commercials have lots of _____, which makes them more appealing or easier to remember than magazine ads. Commercials are usually pretty short although it seems like there sure are a lot of them jammed together. Why is there always music in commercials? Music is easy to remember and must hit people in their _____. The action is important in TV commercials too.

There are many differences in TV commercials and magazine ads, such as length, the use of music, and the use of action.

FREEWRITING EXAMPLE 2

Television commercials have lots of <u>music and action</u>, which makes them more appealing and easier to remember than magazine ads. Commercials are usually short, maybe 15–30 seconds each, although they always seem to be shown five or six at a time. Commercials have music, which is easy to remember and must hit people in their <u>subconscious minds</u>. The action is important in TV commercials too.

1a

In these examples the writer used complete sentences, but you should feel free to write in phrases or even single words. The important thing is to keep writing down all your ideas as quickly as possible without lifting your pen from the paper.

1a-5 Journal Writing

Keeping a **journal,** or a writing notebook, is a practical way to generate ideas about a topic. A journal is different from a diary, which is a list of daily activities. A journal is a collection of ideas or feelings about an observation; descriptions of objects, people, actions, or interactions; random thoughts; and insights that occur to you day to day.

Writing in a journal does not have to take much time, but it should be a daily practice. Writers who spend 10–15 minutes a day writing in their journals discover many ways to use brainstorming, word games, and freewriting to help them develop as writers. To practice, take a topic, any topic, and let your mind wander for 10–15 minutes. Capture all your thoughts on paper.

- Have some fun with your ideas — make lists, play word games (rhyme some words, write opposites).
- Sit outside, close your eyes, listen to the sounds, and then write down everything you've heard.
- Go to a shopping mall, observe people, and write down everything you see.
- Listen to some music, and write down any thoughts, feelings, or impressions that arise.

1a

- Think about a movie or television show you have seen recently. What emotions did you feel while watching the show? What was the show about?
- Write about your favorite person. What qualities make him or her so special?

Eventually, you will begin to feel comfortable putting words on paper. Then when you have to write for an audience other than yourself, you will have the skills you need to begin generating some ideas.

Here are some examples of journal entries.

EXAMPLES FROM JOURNALS

The people in the mall this afternoon were fascinating to watch. Old people, young people, kids — they were all there. Some of the older people were sitting around talking and obviously enjoying each other's company. There were two men watching a rerun of some show on the televisions provided to satisfy husbands of marathon shoppers.

I saw one woman looking at the puppies in the cages in the pet shop and wondered what she was thinking about as she watched the pups jump and bark. She looked rather sad. Was she thinking about buying one of the dogs, or was she remembering a pet she once had? I didn't have the courage to ask her because I felt like I was intruding — maybe I wasn't supposed to notice how unhappy she looked.

I saw several groups of young kids about 10–12 years old — alone and acting weird. A couple of them were smoking and talking like "big shots" while several of them were giggling and talking as fast as they could. I wondered which ones were the ones who knew their parents cared about them.

I also saw a couple, who I guess were married, who looked like they didn't belong at the mall. They looked like they were getting ready to steal something from one of the stores. It occurred to me after watching them for a short time that they were actually cold and were acting like shoppers in order to stay out of the snow. I found myself not only watching this couple but also worrying about them — worrying that someone would chase them out of a store away from the warmth, both physical and emotional, they seemed to need.

Eventually, I saw a man approach them, a man who was using all kinds of hand gestures that literally made my heart and breathing stop. Didn't he know what was going on here? What kind of a coldhearted person was he? I couldn't believe he was actually leading them out of the store, into the mall, away from a little comfort. Then I saw this man take the couple to one of the restaurants inside the mall, say something to the hostess, and hand her some money. After that I decided not to prejudge people, but first I cried.

One of the most beautiful places on earth has to be the Red River Gorge. The gorge has wild rivers, mountains, and spectacular sandstone arches. Try to describe the Red River Gorge to someone who's never been there. It's like trying to describe the beauty of a rainbow to a person who has never seen one.

1a-6 Patterns of Invention

Patterns of invention are ways of thinking that help a writer gather ideas about a topic. Consider the broad topic of music. Let's say you need to write about one particular type of music or one particular song. Here are some ways you can write about it.

- You can *describe* it, what it sounds like, how it makes you feel, and how it is recorded.
- You can *narrate,* or tell, a story about the first time you heard the music or song, about what you are reminded of when you hear it, or about the history behind that type of music or song.
- You can *define* the term *music* or the type of music.
- You can *compare* (show similarities) or *contrast* (show differences) what the music means to you and what it means to someone of a different generation.
- You can explain what *effect* the music has on you and whether or not it might *cause* you to react in a certain way.
- You can *illustrate* the effectiveness of music by giving examples of rhythm, pitch, or volume.
- And you can *classify* the music as big band, rock and roll, heavy metal, or new wave.

Remember that these are simply methods to help you discover what you have to say about a topic. Feel free to use any one

1a

or a combination of them. For examples of paragraphs structured according to the patterns of invention, see section 5d.

1a-7 Interviewing

One of the most practical ways you can gather information is to **interview** people about your topic. Interview knowledgeable people who can share information that might help you focus your ideas for writing.

Think about questions you might have about everyday events: When does the dog go to the vet? How late does the grocery store stay open? How high will the temperature get today? How much damage has been done to the Amazon rain forest? Where are the seal pups located at the zoo? Now, think about how you find the answers. Usually, you ask someone who knows, you read newspapers or magazines, you check an encyclopedia, or you call someone for information.

These questioning techniques work just as well when you need information for writing. Structure questions so that they do not prompt yes/no answers to encourage the people you interview to explain their positions fully. The following general interview questions can be used with most topics.

INTERVIEW QUESTIONS
1. What do you know about the issue?
2. How do you feel about it?
3. Why do you feel that way?
4. How does the issue affect you?
5. How significant is it to you?
6. What do you think people need to know about it?

Often, the information you gather from other people can help you to clarify and focus your own ideas about a topic.

1a-8 Reading Newspapers and Magazines

Try reading newspapers, local as well as nonlocal, for current information on a topic. Generally, newspapers are categorized by size and by the type of information they include. The small newspapers displayed at grocery checkouts are referred to as *tabloid newspapers* and usually contain gossip and sensationalized stories that are neither dependable nor truthful sources of information. The *National Enquirer, Star,* and *Globe* fall into this category. The other type of newspaper, like the one you might have delivered to your home, is usually referred to as an international, national, or local newspaper. This type of newspaper provides a wide assortment of articles on everything from current political, legal, and business news, to fashion, entertainment, and sports news. The *Boston Globe,* the *New York Times,* and the *Los Angeles Times* fall into this category. These newspapers can provide interesting and dependable information on a wide range of current topics. For instance, if the topic is political (like a current congressional race), check the political and editorial sections for ideas. If the topic is related to business (like the status of the stock market), check the business sections for relevant ideas.

Reading magazines is an acceptable method of gathering information to help you generate ideas, but the information published is usually a week or more out of date. Often, people read magazines for opinions or evaluations of topics rather than for current, up-to-the-moment news. For instance, if the topic you are interested in is advertising, the magazine *Advertising Age* will provide a wealth of information on people's ideas about and experiences with advertising. There are literally hundreds of magazines available, ranging from news and business magazines — *Business Week, Time,* and *Newsweek,* for example — to special-interest magazines like *Consumer Reports, Scientific American,* and *Popular Mechanics.*

1a-9 Identifying Editorial Bias

Editorial bias is the particular ethical, philosophical, or political belief stated or implied in newspaper and magazine articles (and in some books). Articles written by editors are usually clearly identified as editorials; however, articles written by contributors often express editorial bias also. The purpose of this kind of writing is to present an opinion on or an argument about a topic or issue (usually controversial) currently on the minds of

1a

the readers. Some professional writers use this type of writing to persuade people to agree with them on a topic or issue.

Critical readers can usually identify editorial bias by carefully evaluating an article. The following questions and discussions can help you to recognize some types of bias.

1. Is a clear distinction made between facts and opinion?
2. If opinions are presented, are they the opinions of experts?

Facts are statements that can be verified — that is, you can find out through research whether or not they are true. **Opinions** are statements of personal belief. The opinion of an expert about his or her area of expertise usually carries more weight than the opinion of someone who is not an expert in that field. Readers assume that the expert has taken into account the relevant facts in forming his or her opinion.

In the following paragraph from a *Time* article called "Condition: Critical," facts are piled up to make the point that American health care costs are already enormous and that they are continuing to grow.

> Americans spend $23,000 a second on medical care, more than $2 billion a day, $733 billion a year. That is nearly twice what they spent seven years ago, including annual increases of 10% during the past two years. For the Federal Government, medical costs have become the fastest-growing major item, increasing at more than 8% annually at a time when inflation is only about 5%. For corporate America, health care has become a crippling expense. General Motors laid out $3.2 billion last year, more than it spent on steel, to provide medical coverage for 1.9 million employees, dependents and retirees. Unchecked, the U.S. medical bill will more than double in the next 10 years, to $1.6 trillion, crowding out spending for other urgent needs. "Health-care costs have created an American state of siege," says Florida Governor Lawton Chiles. "It's going to break us."

The author of this article, Janice Castro, uses facts (in this case, statistics and dollar amounts) to support her idea that Americans spend far too much money on health care. For example, she compares the annual increase in medical costs (8%) to the rate of inflation (5%) to show that medical costs are rising more quickly than other costs. At the end of the paragraph Castro quotes Florida governor Lawton Chiles, who compares health care costs to a "state of siege" and says that these costs are "going to break us." But how much importance should be given to Chiles's opinion? Is he an expert on health care costs? A reader cannot assume that just because a person is an expert in one area, such as government, he or she is an expert in other areas, such as health care costs. While this quotation offers a strong, persuasive conclusion to the paragraph, a reader should be cautious in deciding to adopt Chiles's position on health care costs. The facts given in the article, however, do make Chiles's opinion easier to believe and understand.

The following paragraph is taken from an editorial called "Dear Mr. President . . . ," in which a nurse argues for "putting primary care (of patients) into the hands of nurses." It follows seven other paragraphs that give various reasons for having nurses rather than doctors provide this care.

> Primary care provided by nurses in the schools, workplace, homes, and neighborhood clinics is not a new idea, Mr. President. It's a reformist idea that got squashed by physicians' greed in the early twentieth century. It's important for you to know that physicians have often been spectacularly wrong. For *800 years* they based their notions of human anatomy on Galen's dissection of monkeys (whose interiors differ considerably from humans') because they mistakenly elevated Galen's observations to the level of theology. Use the monkey-dissection test when you're assailed by conventional medical advice on primary health care. Ask: Am I hearing science or theology?

This paragraph uses a combination of fact and opinion to make the points that doctors are greedy and that they make mistakes. Here are two questions you can ask yourself about editorial bias as you examine this paragraph.

3. Does the author support the given opinions with facts?
4. Are all the stated facts relevant to the author's position?

1b

The author states the fact that primary care given by nurses is not a new idea and mentions that in the early twentieth century this idea was "squashed by physicians' greed." She does not give facts to support the statement that it was doctors' greed that kept nurses from giving this care. (Facts may exist to support this claim, but the author does not mention what they are.) She goes on to give an example of doctors' being wrong about basic medical facts. For 800 years doctors based their understanding of human anatomy on their knowledge of monkeys' anatomy. Does this fact support the claim that physicians are greedy? Does it support the writer's overall thesis that nurses should provide primary care to patients? No, it does not. It does make the point that doctors are sometimes wrong and that their knowledge changes over time. However, it avoids the questions "Aren't nurses sometimes wrong too?" and "Doesn't nurses' knowledge also change over time?" In other words, the fact given has nothing to do with the argument that nurses should provide primary care to patients.

The article this paragraph is taken from is clearly labeled "editorial" in the journal it appeared in. Even in news stories, however, check to be sure that fact is clearly separate from opinion, note whether any opinions given are the opinions of authorities in the field of knowledge being discussed, make sure all opinions are supported by facts, and make sure that the facts given are relevant to the writer's overall thesis. Most writing contains some type of bias, whether stated or implied, and readers need to look carefully for that bias and accept it for what it is — opinion.

1b Focusing the Topic

How can you take a topic and narrow it, or **focus** it? Sometimes, you will begin with a general topic, like advertising, animal rights, or health care. The previous explanations about how to generate ideas can also provide ways to examine a topic and pinpoint exactly what areas are specific enough to focus on in a piece of writing. For example, sometimes a topic can be narrowed by taking an item from a brainstorming list and asking some questions about that item. The previous brainstorming list has "liquor ads" as an item that can be focused by asking, "What do I want to say about liquor ads?" or "What particular kind of liquor ads do I want to discuss?" or "What do I want people to know about this topic?" Asking these kinds of questions can help you turn a general idea like "liquor ads" into a more focused idea like "Liquor ads promise companionship" or "Beer ads promise people a good time with friends." The following examples illustrate some general topics that have been focused.

EXAMPLE 1

topic	advertising
focused	car ads
more focused	a specific type of car ad (Honda, Ford, or the like)

EXAMPLE 2

topic	animal rights
focused	animals used in drug testing
more focused	alternatives to using animals in drug testing

EXAMPLE 3

topic	health care
focused	the lack of quality care in hospitals
more focused	quality care in hospitals affected by understaffing

Once you have focused a general topic — that is, made it more specific — you can begin to think about who will read your writing. In the inventing stage of the writing process you wrote for yourself, to discover and explore your ideas about a topic. But most writing is written for others to read. Thinking about your readers, your audience, will help you make decisions about the best way to express your ideas so that others will understand them.

1c   Understanding Audience

In college you will be asked to write for many different types of audiences. Often, the instructor will specify an audience for a writing assignment, and you will need to learn what that audience expects from your writing. What you know about your audience will affect the content, organization, and tone of your writing. Most audiences want direct language that clearly communicates information. As a writer, it is your responsibility to understand the needs of your audience and to communicate information to them as clearly as possible.

As you begin to write, one way to clarify audience needs and expectations is to ask yourself some basic questions that will enable you to better understand who the audience is, how much the audience knows about the topic, and what the audience expects you to explain in your writing. The following checklist provides some questions for you to consider.

AUDIENCE CHECKLIST

1. Who is my audience (fellow students, a friend, a special-interest group, a business professional, or a particular instructor)?
2. What does my audience already know about the topic (the same as me, not as much as me, more than me)?
3. Does my audience have specialized knowledge about the topic?
4. Will I need to simplify information?
5. How does my audience feel about the topic?
6. What would my audience need to know about the topic?
7. What is the most effective way to explain my topic to the audience? Do I need to define, to give examples, to compare, to contrast, to classify, to show causes, to show effects, to persuade, or to explain a process?
8. Will I need to convince the audience that what I say is true?
9. Will I need to give just my point of view, the points of view of others, or both?
10. What would my audience expect me to say about the topic?

Once you ask these questions, even if you have answers for only a few of them, you will have a better sense of your audience and its expectations.

1d   Selecting a Purpose

Your primary **purpose** in any piece of writing is to communicate information or to argue for your point of view about a topic or issue. But underlying that primary purpose is another purpose. Why are you writing this piece? Do you want to describe something? Do you want to narrate or tell a story? Do you want to define an idea? Do you want to compare or contrast two ideas or two items? Do you want to show what causes something to happen or what effect one thing has on another? Do you want to illustrate ideas by giving examples? Do you want to classify or categorize ideas or items? Do you want to inform, to explain, to amuse, to analyze a process, to persuade, or to argue (showing both sides of an issue)? Once you have decided which of these (or which combination) you want to do, you will have selected your purpose for writing a particular piece.

Most instructors will specify a purpose for a writing assignment. First, they may want you to write about some extra reading or research you have done that expands on what you have learned in class. They may have you write for an audience of your peers to see whether you can clearly and effectively present the information you have read or researched. Second, instructors may want you to explain, to a certain group of people, your opinion about something you have learned doing your research. For example, if you have researched a current congressional race, you may be asked to write an editorial about political promises for the campus newspaper. Third, instructors may want to use your writing as a way to measure your understanding of certain information and to measure your ability to communicate this information at a certain level for a particular audience. For instance, if you have read about the use of animals in research, you may be asked to write an article for an animal rights' publication. Fourth, instructors may want to see whether you have under-

1e

stood the information presented in class — they may use your writing to determine your progress in the course.

1e Deciding on a Voice

As a writer, you must find the **voice** that best communicates your ideas. Sometimes, this voice will project a sense of humor; sometimes, it will be very serious. Understanding your audience and your relationship to that audience will help you shape your writing and develop your tone as a writer.

What impression do you want to make on the reader? After you have focused your topic, considered your audience, and selected your purpose, you will need to think about the tone of your writing. Sometimes, when you want to close the distance between yourself and the reader, you will use an informal tone employing pronouns (*I, us, we*) and contractions (*don't, can't, isn't*).

EXAMPLE OF INFORMAL TONE

When I was very young, I remember wondering why people couldn't stand up straight on an icy sidewalk. I can't think of a funnier sight than my neighbor trying to walk his big husky on the ice. The dog wouldn't quit pulling, and the man couldn't stop dancing around like a ballerina on a banana.

This writer brings the reader close by using first-person pronouns and contractions and by assuming that the reader will be able to relate to the humor in the situation described. This informal tone can be effective for many types of writing.

If, however, you want to create distance between yourself and the reader, you may want to use a formal tone. Sometimes, a formal tone does not have first-person pronouns or contractions.

EXAMPLE OF FORMAL TONE

Some people may remember listening to their mothers sing while doing housework. What a pleasant memory this must be for those who can remember, and how sad for those who cannot.

This writer keeps the reader at a distance by giving the reader information about people in general, rather than giving personal information. Again, this formal tone can be effective for many types of writing.

At other times, a formal tone can have first-person pronouns if the writer wants to emphasize his or her responsibility for an opinion, as in the next example. (For more information on levels of formality, see section 9d-1.)

1e

EXAMPLE OF FORMAL TONE WITH FIRST-PERSON PRONOUNS

We need to make ourselves aware of animal rights. We can protect animals from inhumane and cruel treatment in experiments if we join together and boycott certain products and certain foods.

As a writer, you may choose either an informal or a formal tone, depending on your attitude toward the reader, your point of view on the topic, and the distance you want to create between yourself and the reader.

■ A Student Writes

After several class discussions on the issue of censorship, Maggie MacGregor's instructor gave her class the assignment to write a brief essay on some aspect of the topic of censorship. The instructor specified that the audience for the essay would be the other members of the class and that the purpose for the essay would be one of the following:

1. to discuss and illustrate reasons for and against censorship,
2. to inform the audience about some aspect of censorship, or
3. to persuade the audience that censorship is (is not) acceptable.

Maggie began by freewriting on the broad topic of censorship to start generating ideas on the topic.

FREEWRITING

Censorship really bothers me. The government always wants to block what the media presents and always wants to decide what we need to know. I thought the Constitution said something about freedom of the press. I thought that meant we have a right to know everything that goes on in this country. Well, when we don't get all of the information about government policy or government activities, how can they say we have freedom of the press? People in this country have a right to know what is going on.

After she reread what she had written, Maggie decided that this initial reaction to censorship was too negative. It focused too much on the government's keeping information from news organizations. In fact, she couldn't seem to get beyond that idea. So she decided to try to brainstorm some reasons why censorship is a bad idea.

BRAINSTORMING

hides truth
limits information
television — regular and cable — news
newspaper and magazine articles
information into wrong hands
government censorship of top secret ideas
whose decision?
Who has a right to know what information?
age limitations
cultural limitations
Do other governments censor news?
freedom of speech
national security
fairness doctrine
public interest
boundaries — what are limitations of press?
public service
public opinion
objective versus subjective information
Do other governments suppress ideas?
Can people in other countries speak out against their
    leaders?

Maggie realized as she was brainstorming that she actually knew some reasons why censorship is acceptable. Then she revised the list and created two sections: advantages of censorship and disadvantages of censorship.

REVISED LIST

Advantages of Censorship

control of top secret ideas
information into wrong hands
other governments' use of censorship
national security
setting boundaries for media
eliminates speaking out against leaders
controls people

Disadvantages of Censorship

freedom of speech
fairness doctrine
limits information
hides truth
public interest
boundaries not set for media
public service
public opinion
objective versus subjective information

Maggie discovered that she had almost as many reasons for censorship as she had against it. She began to realize that in at least one case, national security, censorship seemed necessary and possibly more important than the public's right to know. She thought that before deciding on a focused topic and purpose, she had better list other questions that occurred to her.

QUESTIONS TO CONSIDER

1. How is television news affected by government censorship?
2. Who decides what to censor?
3. Who has a right to know what information?
4. What should be the limitations of the media?
5. Should the media have access to all government information?

Once Maggie looked over her brainstorming lists and questions, she realized that her main interest was the conflict between the advantages and disadvantages of government censorship. She thought that other members of her class may have shared her initial dislike of censorship and that her purpose in writing this essay could be to show that in some very specific cases censorship makes sense. She refocused the topic to make it a little more specific.

> FOCUSED TOPIC   Advantages and disadvantages of government censorship

After further thinking Maggie realized that different groups censor particular categories of information. For example, some groups don't think that sexually explicit art should be shown in art galleries or museums. Some news organizations don't broadcast violent film footage or publish photographs of graphic violence. And some parents restrict their children to certain forms of entertainment: specific movies, video games, or music. However, Maggie decided to focus her essay on government suppression of information, and so she revised her topic to focus it further.

> MORE FOCUSED TOPIC   Advantages and disadvantages of government censorship of information

Then Maggie looked at her earlier freewriting, her brainstorming, and her questions to find all the ideas that related to her more focused topic. For easy reference she listed them in two columns with new headings for better organization of her original ideas.

IDEAS FOR FOCUSED TOPIC

Reasons for Censorship

control of top secret information
age limitations
information into wrong hands
cultural limitations
other governments' use of censorship
national security

setting boundaries for media
eliminates speaking out against leaders
controls people
television news coverage limited
controls media

Reasons against Censorship

freedom of speech
fairness doctrine
limits information
hides truth
public interest
media boundaries unreasonable
public service
public opinion
objective versus subjective information
people's right to know

 # A Classmate Responds

Maggie's instructor suggested to the students that at various points during the writing process they should get feedback from each other. Taking this suggestion, Maggie asked one of her classmates to respond to her lists of reasons for and against government censorship. She wanted to know if her classmate Miguel could help her think of any other ideas to include in her lists. Maggie and Miguel worked together and came up with a few more ideas.

ADDITIONAL IDEAS

Reasons for Censorship

withholding information about military strategies
    or capabilities
withholding information about terrorist tactics
freedom of press and limitations
president's constitutional privilege to withhold information

Reasons against Censorship

use of censorship by governments in Asian and European
    countries
media's right to profit from news

Maggie finally felt ready to write a very rough draft of the ideas she had thought of so far. Her discovery draft is reprinted at the end of chapter 2.

Chapter 2

Drafting the Essay

Sometimes, the most productive way to begin a piece of writing is to jump right in and let ideas flow. Some writers find the inventing techniques discussed in chapter 1 helpful, but others feel more comfortable writing an entire draft to discover what they know about—or their attitude toward—their topic. Then they go back and look at what they have written to see what information they can use in their essay.

2a Writing a Discovery Draft

Most writers don't know exactly what they want to say about a topic until they start writing; the act of writing helps shape their ideas. Writing a discovery draft is one way of finding out what you want to say about your topic. A **discovery draft** gives you the freedom to write down your ideas in any order. For example, you can write the middle of the essay before you write the beginning, or you can write straight through from beginning to end. Later, you can organize your ideas in a way that readers will understand.

The following discovery drafts use the topics of music and animal rights.

EXAMPLE 1

Music has always been a part of my life. My first memories of music are those involving people who I thought were great musicians. I remember as a child listening to the organ music at Mass, wondering if I would ever be able to play an instrument that well. I also remember listening to my father play the piano

27

2a

for hours at a time, envying his talent. He loved "taking requests" and could play any song a person could hum for him. He never had lessons; he simply had the ability to "play by ear."

While in elementary school, I listened to all of the popular music played on the radio — rock and roll, hard rock, and heavy metal — and decided that I wanted to learn how to play the guitar. After a lot of begging and pleading, I convinced my parents to buy me a guitar — a cheap one. Thus began my own real journey into the world of music. My parents could not afford to pay for lessons (for what seemed to them a whim on my part), so I experimented with sounds until I could pick out string combinations that sounded like music.

I continued my practicing throughout high school, and eventually I learned that I could do more than just play music. I could even write it. My parents were so pleased with my progress that they bought me an incredible-sounding acoustic guitar that I still have. Listening to music suddenly was more than just a pastime. In fact, it became the most cherished aspect of my life.

EXAMPLE 2

Animal rights is an issue that fascinates me and frightens me. It fascinates me because there are so many different groups of people that want everyone to know what happens to animals raised for food. These groups say we should boycott certain meats like veal because of the inhumane ways the cows are treated.

I get frightened when I think about the ways animals are used to test drugs and chemicals used in cosmetics. When the animals are used in lab experiments, they are treated cruelly and are tortured. For example, rabbits are used to test chemicals used in eye makeup. Chemicals are put into the rabbit's eyes, which are then taped shut. If the chemicals don't harm the rabbit's eyes, they are considered to be safe to put in the makeup for humans.

What can people do to stop this cruelty? Will it really matter if we simply stop eating a certain kind of meat or stop buying a particular brand of makeup? Some products even carry labels that say no animals were used to test the product.

Notice that although these drafts are not perfect, they do communicate the writers' initial ideas about their topics. To revise the first discovery draft into a form that readers can understand, the writer needs to ask what the purpose of the essay is. The draft needs more information in each paragraph to clearly communicate that purpose to the audience. The second discovery draft needs more examples of the main points the writer is trying to make. Chapter 3 will show you ways to revise your drafts.

2b The Parts of an Essay

Before you think about revising your brainstorming, free-writing, or discovery draft into a form that readers will understand, you should become familiar with how the parts of an essay function. The following sections describe each part.

The Introduction

The introduction in an essay sets the context for the reader. The purpose of this paragraph (or group of paragraphs) is to let the reader know what ideas you plan to discuss and how you plan to discuss them. In other words, you give the reader some kind of commitment. And you want to do so without saying "This essay is about so and so, and I plan to discuss it this way." You do not need to tell the reader in those exact words what you are going to do. Instead, you use one of several approaches to suggest what you intend to discuss and how you will discuss it. So you will choose an approach that helps you give the reader a commitment you can keep.

For example, in an essay on advertising you might choose to begin in one of the following ways:

ASK A QUESTION

How can businesses effectively sell their products? Obviously, they need a way to get the consumer's attention; this is the purpose of ads. In hard economic times, people do not want to spend money. Advertising people know this and, thus, use various approaches in their attempts to get the public to buy products. Through close examination of one ad's techniques, people can learn to understand how advertisements work. Techniques like imagery, use of language, and use of color present the idea of reward and appeal to a person's "hidden needs."

2b

SET A SCENE

While thumbing through a popular magazine recently, I ran across a cigarette advertisement that really caught my eye. Obviously, the main objective of the company presenting the advertisement is to catch the consumer's attention so that the product will be on the consumer's mind and, therefore, get purchased. However, as I looked further, I noticed that some ads were more appealing to my senses than others seemed to be. I then decided to examine this particular cigarette ad more closely to see exactly what made it appeal to me so much.

GIVE BACKGROUND INFORMATION

Since the turn of the century, companies have tried to sell their products to the buying public. These companies have tried various ways to promote their products and have sought the advice of sociologists and psychologists in an effort to find out what makes people respond favorably to a sales pitch.

However you decide to introduce your topic, make sure that your audience will understand the main point you will be making in your essay.

2b-2 Writing a Thesis Statement

The controlling or guiding idea in a piece of writing can often be written in the form of a topic sentence (for a paragraph) or a thesis statement (for an essay). A **topic sentence** or **thesis statement** tells the reader what you will discuss and gives both the writer and the reader a clear direction to follow. (For more information on topic sentences, see section 5a.)

Sometimes, you will know what your thesis is before you begin to write an essay. For example, your instructor may give this assignment: "Discuss three reasons people should not smoke cigarettes." In this case, once you have decided on the three reasons you will discuss, the thesis statement needs only to be spelled out: "People should not smoke cigarettes because smoking leads to cancer, it is harmful to others who don't smoke themselves, and it is addictive."

Other times, you will need to figure out the exact focus you want to take in your writing by brainstorming, freewriting, or writing a discovery draft. Ideally, you should at least have an idea for a thesis before you select details for your essay. And as you revise your drafts, you will probably need to revise your thesis statement to reflect your changing ideas. The following guidelines will help you write a thesis statement.

2b

1. The thesis should focus on what the writer wants to explain about the topic and should meet the needs of the audience.

   As you consider your thesis, ask yourself what kinds of explanation are needed. Think about how much explanation the audience will need to clearly understand your point. Then write your thesis considering the amount of detail you must provide for your audience.
   Here is an acceptable thesis for a general audience.

   Some music, like big band or heavy metal, is easy to classify according to its appeal to a specific age group.

   This thesis is acceptable for an audience that expects an essay providing a general way of classifying music. A more select audience will have different expectations.
   Here is an acceptable thesis for an audience of classical music lovers.

   Bach was self-taught as a musician and composer to the extent that he studied, transcribed, and arranged the music of various composers so that he could learn from them and develop his own particular style.

   This thesis statement is acceptable for an audience that enjoys classical music and that would be interested in more information about a particular composer.
   Finally, here is an acceptable thesis for an audience of music majors.

   The harpsichord differs from the piano in its clear, crisp sound and its consistent volume.

   This last thesis statement is acceptable for an audience that expects an essay that discusses in some detail the differences between two particular instruments.

2b

2. The thesis should be general enough to require supporting details but specific enough for the length of the writing.

After some preliminary brainstorming or freewriting on the topic (in this case, music), you can begin to examine what aspect of music you would like to discuss. Part of your brainstorming list might look like the following example.

BRAINSTORMING

classical	rock
baroque	heavy metal
German composers	British composers
harpsichord	guitars
strings	synthesizers

The items in this list are broad topics or subjects that need to be made much more specific to create effective thesis statements. Let your areas of interest guide you in selecting which items you want to pursue. Perhaps you are more interested in classical music than modern music, and perhaps a particular German composer interests you. For example, let's assume you are interested in writing about the German composer Johann Sebastian Bach. You might have the following preliminary thoughts for thesis statements.

POSSIBILITIES FOR THESIS DEVELOPMENT

1. Bach was a German composer who was self-taught.
2. Bach was one of many composers writing during the early eighteenth century.
3. Bach wrote a lot of compositions during his lifetime.
4. Bach learned from studying and transcribing the works of other composers.
5. Bach transcribed opus 3, no. 3, for violin and orchestra by Vivaldi.

The first four ideas are too general to be covered in a brief essay. Each of these statements would require many pages for a full development. When a thesis is too

2b

general, you will have trouble focusing your ideas and deciding what to write. The fifth attempt presents a fact — a statement that cannot be supported by other details because, as a fact, it is not arguable. With a thesis statement this specific you will have difficulty finding enough information to develop a paragraph. The first four ideas, however, with revision, do present possibilities for a focused thesis statement.

To decide which possible thesis statement to revise, make a list of details relevant to the thesis to determine whether you have enough (or too much) information for a short essay. From these details you can choose several to help you focus the thesis. For example, you may have written that Bach was in many ways self-taught; he transcribed Vivaldi scores; he was born in 1685 and died in 1750; he arranged the music of other composers; he was intent on developing his own style as a composer and as a musician. From this list you can choose details to add to your thesis to make it acceptable.

ACCEPTABLE THESIS

Bach was in many ways self-taught as a musician and composer; he studied, transcribed, and arranged the music of various composers so that he could learn from them and develop his own particular style.

The body of this essay will discuss how Bach studied, transcribed, and arranged music to develop his own particular style.

3. The thesis should clearly reflect the writer's point of view on the topic.

Here is a thesis that presents an obvious point of view.

OBVIOUS POINT OF VIEW

Classical music is important because it is relaxing, it soothes the nerves, and it refreshes the soul.

The next thesis presents an implied point of view.

2b

IMPLIED POINT OF VIEW

Bach was in many ways self-taught as a musician and composer; he studied, transcribed, and arranged the music of various composers so that he could learn from them and develop his own particular style.

This thesis statement implies the writer's point of view in the second part, where the writer gives an interpretation of how and why Bach was self-taught.

2b-3   Placing the Thesis Statement

The thesis statement is usually part of the introduction to the essay. It clearly specifies the idea(s) that the writer plans to discuss in the essay. For instance, in the first two examples in section 2b-1 (under the headings "Ask a Question" and "Set a Scene"), the thesis statement is the last sentence in each introductory paragraph. Notice how each thesis spells out the writer's plan.

The thesis may also tell the reader the order in which the writer plans to discuss his or her ideas, as in the example of advertising techniques. The body paragraphs of this essay will discuss first imagery, then language, and finally color in support of the thesis statement.

While the thesis statement is often the last sentence of the introduction, it can be placed wherever the writer thinks it fits logically. Notice the placement of the thesis in the discovery draft in example 1 of section 2a. The first paragraph of that example is repeated here.

EXAMPLE 1

Music has always been a part of my life. My first memories of music are those involving people who I thought were great musicians. I remember as a child listening to the organ music at Mass, wondering if I would ever be able to play an instrument that well. I also remember listening to my father play the piano for hours at a time, envying his talent. He loved "taking requests" and could play any song a person could hum for him. He never had lessons; he simply had the ability to "play by ear."

In this example the placement of the thesis at the beginning of the introduction is appropriate and logical because it implies that the essay will be narrative and because it tells the direction the essay will take. It will start with examples from the writer's early years and continue through her elementary and high school years. Placement at the end of the introduction would have caused a break in the flow of ideas.

2b-4 The Body

The **body** of an essay discusses the ideas mentioned in the thesis, in the same order. The body of an essay can be developed in many ways, including any combination of the following techniques.

2b-4a Definitions of the Ideas Presented

If you are writing about specific issues like abortion, animal rights, euthanasia, or anything that carries emotional as well as objective meanings, you need to define your terms. When you give a dictionary definition, your own definition, a commonly accepted definition, or some combination of them, you clarify for your reader exactly how you intend to use the terms.

2b-4b Generalizations with Details for Support

Regardless of the type of essay you write, you should provide in your paragraphs general statements about the topic with specific details to support the generalizations. In an essay on advertising, for instance, if you make a generalization like "Makeup advertisers use famous people to promote products," then you need to provide specific details like "Makeup company X uses ads with famous models like Ms. Y."

2b-4c Examples and Illustrations

In most essays you will need to give examples to clarify, to explain, and to support your ideas. In an essay on animal rights, if you say that animals are mistreated in lab experiments, then

2b

you need to illustrate how they are mistreated by giving examples of the ways they are handled in specific types of experiments.

2b-4d Comparisons and Contrasts

In some essays you may find that in order to clarify an issue, you need to compare or contrast the issue with a different issue. In an essay on a current congressional race, for example, you might want to show how similar and how different the candidates were.

2b-4e Causes and Effects

Sometimes, you may have a topic that can best be discussed by explaining its causes and its effects. In an essay on euthanasia you may want to discuss what causes people to consider euthanasia and what effects it has on family members and friends.

2b-4f Classifications

When you classify people or things, you show how they are like the other members of the group they belong to and how they are different from people or things that belong to other groups. Thus, if you are writing about political campaigns, you may find it helpful to classify or categorize the candidates. You may use simple classifications (Democratic, Republican, Independent, Socialist) or complex classifications (liberal, conservative, right wing, left wing). When using classification, be sure to define all your terms clearly.

2b-4g Analyses

In many essays you will want to examine the topic as closely as possible by literally "picking it apart." You may want to define an issue, examine how others interpret it, explain how you interpret it, and then put all of the ideas together to emphasize how complex or how difficult the issue is.

Whichever of these approaches you choose, the body of your essay should develop and support each general statement with specific examples. Remember that if you list ideas in your thesis statement, then you should arrange the body paragraphs in the same order that you present those ideas in the thesis.

2b-5 The Conclusion

The purpose of the **conclusion** is to clarify, to emphasize, or to illustrate the connection among all the major ideas that you have presented in your essay. Notice the different effects of the approaches presented in the following conclusions.

2b-5a Summary

This type of conclusion restates or summarizes the main ideas in the essay.

SUMMARY CONCLUSION

Obviously, this product "demands more than the ordinary." Through fantasy and ambiguity the advertiser entices consumers to look inside the closed door in the ad to see if it reveals the sense they perceive by glancing over the ad. The advertisers have shown quite effectively in their layout that their product does more than the average product. The tools they have utilized effectively attract the reader.

2b-5b Thesis Restatement

This type of conclusion repeats the thesis statement and then emphasizes its importance.

THESIS RESTATEMENT CONCLUSION

A successful ad sells the product. By effectively using the illusion of a refreshing taste, color and color symbolism, layout, and stereotypes in this ad, the advertiser persuades the consumer to purchase the product. Since the sale of cigarettes continues to increase each year, obviously the result of effective advertising, one can consider this ad a success.

2b-5c Call to Action

This type of conclusion asks and encourages the reader to react to what has been discussed in the essay.

2c

CALL TO ACTION CONCLUSION

Obviously, advertisers will use deceptive means to lure consumers and to convince them that one particular product is better than others. People need to understand what advertisers try to do, and they need to learn how to become careful and not gullible consumers. People need to realize that advertisers will promise beauty, wealth, companionship, youth, and immortality just to catch people's attention. And people need to remember that most advertisers make promises they cannot keep.

There are many other types of conclusions that writers may use, depending on the topic and the purpose of the essay. They may use a suggestion for a new way to view the topic, which asks the reader to consider a new (or at least a different) perspective on the topic. They may use a prediction for the future, which asks the reader to consider the information in the essay as support for what could happen in the future. They may use a solution to a problem, which provides a possible answer (or answers) to a problem discussed in the essay. They may present alternatives in a conclusion that explain choices other than those discussed in the essay. Or they may use a series of rhetorical questions, questions intended to make the reader think.

Regardless of the type of conclusion you choose, try to link the information in it to the thesis without restating exactly what you have presented in the introduction. Do not introduce new ideas in the conclusion; instead, end with a clear, final statement.

Now that you understand the function of each part of an essay and know some strategies for drafting the introduction, the body, and the conclusion, you may want to use a working outline to decide on a logical way to present your ideas to your readers.

2c   Using a Working Outline

A **working outline** is a preliminary, structured plan for a writer to follow. You can use a simple, three-part working outline for writing a first draft.

Let's look at the topic of animal rights again. You can begin by brainstorming or freewriting to generate some ideas on the topic. For example, while brainstorming, you may come up with the following ideas. Animal rights is an issue people are concerned about now; there are animal rights activists and foes; animals are used for research by cosmetic companies and university labs; animals there are mistreated; animals raised for food are mistreated; people can be cruel. You can then make a simple outline to help you organize some of these ideas.

2c

SIMPLE OUTLINE FOR ANIMAL RIGHTS ESSAY

INTRODUCTION
1. What are the rights of animals?
2. Why is this an issue now?
3. How do most people feel about this issue?
4. What do special-interest groups say about the issue?
5. State a thesis — an opinion statement or declaration about the issue. (See section 2b-2 for an explanation of thesis.)

BODY
1. Give examples of how animals are treated in lab experiments.
2. Give examples of how animals raised for food are treated.

CONCLUSION
1. What is significant about this issue?
2. What can we learn about ourselves in relation to how we perceive the treatment of animals?
3. What do people need to know about animal rights?

As another example, suppose you have been asked to write about problems in the American health care system. After some initial brainstorming, you have the following list of ideas.

BRAINSTORMING LIST FOR HEALTH CARE ESSAY

costly
sometimes don't hear horror stories
need good insurance
hospitals expensive
some hospitals better than others
some health care people as gods
Medicare
nursing homes

abuse of the elderly
cost of medicine
name-brand versus generic drugs
hospitals understaffed
nurses overworked
doctors overpaid

The next step in writing an essay is to categorize these ideas (cost of care, horror stories, quality of care). Then you can use the categories to put together a brief three-part outline to decide what you want to say in the introduction, the body, and the conclusion. Here is one possibility.

OUTLINE FOR HEALTH CARE ESSAY BY CATEGORIES

INTRODUCTION
1. Explain how most people view our health care system.
2. How do the media present the health care system to us?
3. What areas get favorable or unfavorable press?
4. What area is of interest to you and why? [thesis]

BODY
1. Explain what you know about the area of your interest.
2. What have you read about it; what have you actually experienced?
3. Give examples.

CONCLUSION
1. How do you feel about the issue?
2. What do people need to know about the issue?

Another possibility is to write topic sentences and use them in the three-part outline. The following outline shows topic sentences that incorporate ideas from the brainstorming list.

OUTLINE FOR HEALTH CARE ESSAY BY TOPIC SENTENCES

INTRODUCTION
1. Most people know that the health care system has problems, but they don't realize just how many problems exist until they are hospitalized.
2. People hear good things about health care, but they don't always hear the horror stories.
3. There are some problem areas like understaffing in hospitals. [thesis]

BODY
1. Although some hospitals are nonprofit, hospitalization is expensive, even if people have good insurance policies.
2. Hospitals are understaffed, and nurses often have to work 12- or 16-hour shifts.
3. Understaffing is dangerous for patients but cost-effective for hospitals.

CONCLUSION
1. Hospitals need to find ways to cut costs for patients.
2. Hospitals also need to find ways to provide better care for patients.
3. People need to be aware that hospitals are businesses interested in making a profit.

2c

Some of the items from the brainstorming list were not used in this outline, but they could have been used in an essay on the costs of health care, on the costs of medicines, or on nursing homes. However, each of the ideas used was made into a topic sentence that, with the use of examples for support, could be developed into a paragraph. Using this approach to writing a first draft, you can respond to your ideas as you think of them and then organize them into an outline.

There are many approaches to writing early drafts. If you already have your own effective method for writing a first draft and feel comfortable with the method, stay with it. If not, experiment with different strategies until you find a process that works for you.

■ A Student Writes

Once Maggie finished brainstorming with Miguel, she felt comfortable enough to write a discovery draft to examine her ideas and to find out what she really wanted to say about the topic of censorship.

DISCOVERY DRAFT

What Happens If the US Government Censors the News?

US censorship of the news media involves censoring information that pertains to national security, which includes limiting the public's right to know. In a democracy people usually have a right to know what their government is doing in domestic as well as foreign affairs. Sometimes, however, the government needs to ensure that certain information does not fall into the wrong hands.

One of the amendments to the Constitution lists freedom of the press as a right for citizens in this country. Most people are used to turning on the news on television or reading the newspaper to find out what is happening in this country and around the world. Although these two sources of information are considered to be public services, they are profitable businesses. Who would profit from limitations being put on the broadcast or publication of news?

Sometimes, the government censors information to protect national security. Since news is broadcast worldwide, people in the states as well as people overseas get up-to-the-minute reports on news stories that used to take hours to transmit. If everyone sees these broadcasts, information the American government does not want known internationally needs to be withheld — censored.

What about the American people's right to know what is going on in the government? People in this country have a right to know what the government is doing, but do they have a right to know every single detail? What are the limitations, and who has a right to set them? Just how much do people have a right to know?

What about how much information is censored here in the states compared to what is censored in other countries?

Obviously, there are reasons for and against the issue of government censorship of news. People need to realize that what they hear and read is limited to a certain extent and that it may not include information that the government deems inappropriate to provide.

Maggie's instructor encouraged the students to continue to get feedback from each other and provided them with a series of handouts of questions to be used at each point in the drafting process. So Maggie asked Miguel to read her draft and give her some suggestions based on the questions the instructor provided.

☑ A Classmate Responds

QUESTIONS FOR REVIEW

1. Is the writer's thesis stated?
2. What is the main point of the draft?
3. What is your favorite part of the draft?
4. What parts make you want to know more?

Miguel's responses gave Maggie some helpful hints.

MIGUEL'S RESPONSES

1. The thesis is not stated, but I think you're talking about how difficult it is to decide whether government censorship is good or bad.
2. The main point is that the government censors information to protect people, not to hurt them.
3. I like the part about the Constitution.
4. I want to know more about the Constitution versus people's right to know everything. I also want to know what you mean by the difference between censoring news and censoring information. Give examples of what the government doesn't want other countries to know and how information is censored in other countries.

■ A Student Writes

After putting the draft aside for a day and keeping Miguel's suggestions in mind, Maggie reread what she had written to see what her main focus should be. She decided that the thesis for her essay should clearly state her opinion on the issue of government censorship of information.

THESIS

The American government often censors information for national security reasons and not necessarily to infringe upon the public's right to know.

Then Maggie was ready to draft an outline on the basis of what she had written, what Miguel had suggested, and what she wanted to explain.

OUTLINE DRAFT

INTRODUCTION
 1. Discuss censorship.
 2. State thesis.
BODY
 1. Give reasons for.
 2. Give reasons against.
CONCLUSION
 1. Should the government censor?
 2. List alternatives, if any.

After writing this basic structure, Maggie was ready to expand the draft of the outline. Her revised outline is reprinted at the end of chapter 3.

Chapter 3

Revising the Draft

The biggest worry some students have is that they try to write perfectly in the first draft. They try to get each sentence perfect and each word spelled correctly when they first put them on the page. This way of writing becomes very frustrating. You should not worry about doing any editing (correcting errors) until you get to the final draft of your essay. If your paper goes through several drafts, you may end up eliminating some troublesome areas. So why waste your time struggling with sentence structure or looking up words in the dictionary when you can be generating new ideas? You can always correct your errors before you copy the final draft. Concentrate on getting your ideas down on paper; you can reorganize ideas and correct errors later.

The most effective way to revise is to distance yourself as much as possible from the draft. After writing the draft, leave it alone for as long as you can — several hours, overnight, preferably a few days. If time is a problem, type the draft to gain some distance from it. When you are ready to read the draft again, first make sure it says everything you want to say about the topic, keeping in mind your audience and your purpose. Add or delete information if necessary. Second, try to imagine how your audience will react to it. If possible, have a friend or classmate read your writing and give you feedback on its content, organization, and effectiveness. The "Global Revision Checklist" in section 3d offers questions to think about as you reread your draft.

3a Expanding Ideas

One way to rethink your first ideas is to take each paragraph and see whether it covers and explains a single part of your

3a

three-part outline. (The three parts are the introduction, body, and conclusion.) Another is to outline the draft *after* you write it to see whether it is logical and complete. As you examine the ideas presented in your paragraphs, see whether you have given ideas that are too general to explain exactly what you mean. If so, you will need to focus them and add examples for support.

EXAMPLE 1

Too General

Music is relaxing.

General Statement Needing Support

Natalie Cole's songs have soft music that can relax anyone.

Examples for Support

In her song "Unforgettable," she sings a duet with her father, Nat King Cole. The slow rhythm and soft tones of this song can make everyone from teens to senior citizens feel warm and relaxed.

EXAMPLE 2

Too General

Cigarette ads are soothing.

General Statement Needing Support

This cigarette ad has pastel colors that soothe the reader.

Examples for Support

The blue sky combined with the green trees in the background will have a tranquil effect on the average reader.

You can expand on general ideas with this type of revising by adding examples, illustrations, descriptive details, and statistics.

You need to think about your audience and purpose again at this point. How much information will your audience need to understand the points you are trying to make? You also need to keep your purpose in mind so that you can present your ideas clearly. If your purpose is to describe, check to see whether you have used concrete, vivid details. If your purpose is to define, make sure you have clarified your terminology. If your purpose is to explain, check to see whether you have included specific, clear examples. If your purpose is to compare or to contrast, make sure you have distinguished between similarities and differences. If your purpose is to classify, check to see whether you have presented and defined your categories clearly and concisely. If your purpose is to persuade, make sure you have clearly stated your position on the topic or issue. If your purpose is to explain a process, check to be sure that each step of the process is included in the correct order.

3b

3b Reorganizing Ideas

As you rethink your original draft, you may also decide to change the order of the ideas you include. Think of reorganizing as putting together a puzzle. The parts of your essay should fit together smoothly and form a clear picture for your readers.

As an example, look at the following outline for one paragraph of a first draft. The topic is why people going to a foreign country should know the local language and customs.

OUTLINE

Tentative Topic Sentence

Knowing the language allows business travelers and vacationers to do some basic things they take for granted in their own country.

1. Business travelers need to know the language.
   a. They have to be able to find their way around, which could be complicated if they don't know at least some phrases in the language.
   b. They may need to find a place to live if they are going to work in the country for a while.
   c. They may need to make business phone calls in the local language.

3b

2. Vacation travelers need to know the language.

a. They need to find out how to get to local attractions such as museums or theaters.

b. They may have to use the phone to make dinner reservations at fancy restaurants.

c. They may want to communicate with the local people just to feel like they are in a friendly place.

The writer of this outline had intended to talk about the different reasons business travelers and vacationers should learn the language of the country they are going to. But as she examined the outline, she noticed that the reasons both groups of travelers need to know the language were the same — or similar enough to make the division into business people and vacationers meaningless. She also realized that she didn't have enough examples to make her point clearly. At the same time she thought that she should expand on some of her ideas to make them more specific and concrete. Finally, she had to revise the topic sentence once she had decided on her new plan. Her revised outline follows.

REVISED OUTLINE

Revised Topic Sentence

Knowing the language allows travelers to do some basic things they take for granted in their own country.

1. Travelers need to be able to find their way around.

a. They need to be able to read street signs and maps.

b. They may need to ask directions.

2. Travelers who want to understand the local situation or conditions may want to read the newspaper.

3. Travelers may need to use the phone, to shop, or to eat in restaurants, and knowing the language will help make that easier.

4. Travelers may want to make friends with some local people.

a. They may be lonely being away from home.

b. They may just enjoy making friends.

c. They may want to understand more about the people who are around them.

By reorganizing her outline, the writer improved the flow of ideas in her paragraph. (The finished paragraph is in the sample paper "Living in a Foreign Country" in chapter 4.)

Revising your outline can give you a clearer sense of the direction of your essay. It may also help you identify the most logical organization for your ideas.

Once you have given reorganization some thought, you are ready to write your second draft. One way to check your ideas before writing this second draft is to see whether you have done what you planned to do. Write your thesis statement on a separate piece of paper and check it against every paragraph you have written. If a paragraph in some way explains, expands, or develops the thesis, then the paragraph belongs in the essay. If a paragraph has nothing to do with the thesis statement, then you need to omit the paragraph or rework it so that it does relate to the thesis. You can also check each paragraph to see whether it has a topic sentence (see section 5a) and a concluding statement.

3c   Connecting Ideas

A **transition** is a word or phrase that makes a logical connection between ideas. Transitions are signals for readers to follow; they help readers move smoothly from one idea to another idea. One way to check for transitions is to write down the first sentence of each paragraph. These sentences should follow logically and tell you exactly what your paper says in a short paragraph. If the sentences don't follow logically, you have left out some transitions.

Think about what you do when you speak before an audience. You let your audience know when your ideas shift into a new paragraph by using a transition: "Oh, there's one more thing I want to mention." Other signals you use in speaking include a change of inflection (emphasis on words), a change in body language, and a change of facial expression to let listeners know when you plan to shift your focus.

Since you cannot use these physical cues in writing, you need to use other types of cues to make clear transitions (or

3c

connections) between ideas and between paragraphs in your es-say. But think about the cues you use for shifts of focus in speak-ing to help you decide where you need transitions in your essay and which transitions to use. For further guidance, notice the transitions used in the paragraph examples in section 5e. The following chart gives some helpful transitions you may want to consider.

TRANSITIONS

1. words and phrases that announce a *conclusion* or *summary*

accordingly	hence
as a result	in conclusion
lastly	in short
finally	in summary
consequently	in general
obviously	therefore
clearly	to sum up
in fact	

2. words and phrases that announce items of *equal emphasis*

again	another
also	as well as
and	likewise
furthermore	
moreover	

3. words and phrases that announce an *example* or an *illustration*

for example	in such cases
for instance	in the same manner
in other words	just as
namely	the following
specifically	to illustrate
thus	

4. words and phrases that indicate a *change of direction*

although	in spite of
despite	notwithstanding
instead	regardless

5. words and phrases that call attention to *important ideas*

note	notice
observe	of significance

6. words and phrases that designate a *similarity*

likewise	similarly
just as	like

7. words and phrases that designate a *contrast*

but	nevertheless
still	meanwhile
however	otherwise
yet	instead
regardless	whereas
despite	while
on the other hand	unlike
on the contrary	

8. words and phrases that add another *circumstance* or *aspect*

likewise	in addition
similarly	moreover
second	next
finally	again
or	now
besides	

9. *all-inclusive* words and phrases

entirely	under all circumstances
only	at all times
always	every

10. *negative words*

no	none
never	not
neither	nor

3d   Revision Checklist

Revision means to reenvision or to rethink what you have written — *not just to recopy it.* When you revise, first look at the piece of writing as a whole to make sure that the thesis is precise and accurate, that each paragraph clearly relates to the thesis, and that the organization is effective and logical. These corrections

3d

are called "global revisions." Once you've made changes in these larger elements, you can make changes in the smaller elements, such as sentence structure, word use, grammar, punctuation, and mechanics. Use the following checklist to organize your revision process.

GLOBAL REVISION CHECKLIST

Content
1. Is the information true and accurate?
2. Do any ideas need further explanation?
3. Should information be added or omitted?
4. Is the information understandable?

Organization
1. Does the draft have three distinct parts: introduction, body, and conclusion?
2. Is there a thesis statement in the introduction? Does it accurately reflect the content of the essay?
3. Does each paragraph have a topic sentence that relates to the thesis statement?
4. Does each paragraph have ideas that reflect the topic sentence?
5. Does each paragraph make a generalization and then offer details that support it?
6. Is each paragraph clearly organized?
7. Does the conclusion really end the draft, or does it inadvertently start a new topic?
8. Do the paragraphs follow each other logically and coherently?

Purpose
1. Does this draft satisfy the criteria for the assignment (to describe, to narrate, to define, to compare and to contrast, to show cause and effect, to illustrate a process, to classify, to persuade, to argue)?
2. Is the purpose of the draft clear?
3. Does it satisfy your need to present information in a specific way?

Audience
1. Does the draft address the correct audience?
2. Does it have an appropriate tone or point of view?
3. Is enough information given considering what the audience may or may not know about the topic?

4. Is the language usage (style) appropriate?
5. How will the information presented make the reader think, or feel, or react?

3e   Checking Sentences and Words

Next, look at sentence variety. Do you have a variety of simple as well as compound and complex sentences? (For an explanation of sentence variety, see section 6b.) Finally, look at word usage. Does each word say exactly what you mean? Would the audience understand and feel comfortable reading the words you have chosen? For example, have you used slang when standard English would be more appropriate? (For information about word use, see chapter 9.) After you read through the second draft to see whether it is logical, coherent (Does it make sense?), and cohesive (Are all the ideas related?), you are ready to proofread and edit.

■   A Student Writes

In order to expand her outline, Maggie needed to rethink her thesis in terms of what ideas would illustrate, expand, and support the thesis. She wanted to address as clearly as possible points that would provide her readers with an understanding of the complexity of the issue. She decided to use a detailed outline as a structure for the development of her ideas.

REVISED OUTLINE

INTRODUCTION
1. What does government censorship mean?
2. What is the difference between censoring information and censoring news?
   a. Give examples of government censorship in the states.

b. Give examples of government censorship in other
countries.
3. Why does the American government censor
information?

BODY
1. What are the public's constitutional rights concerning
censorship?
2. What advantages are there to government censorship
of information?
3. What disadvantages are there?
4. Why does the government want some information to
be unavailable?

CONCLUSION
1. Does the government have a right to censor information?
a. When?
b. Why?
2. What alternatives are there to this type of censorship?
3. What do people need to know about government
censorship?

Using her revised outline, Maggie revised her discovery
draft. In this revised draft she tried to follow her outline closely
and give as many examples as she could. Where she could not
immediately think of examples, she left bracketed reminders so
that she could later add some examples for support.

REVISED DRAFT

Why Does the US Government Censor Information?

US government censorship of information involves censoring
official secrets that ensure national security, which includes limiting the public's right to know about foreign and domestic policies. In a democracy people usually have a right to know what
their government is doing in domestic as well as foreign affairs.
Sometimes, however, the government needs to ensure that certain information does not fall into the wrong hands. Differentiating between government censorship of information and
government control of the news media helps to clarify the distinction between what people need to know and what they have
a right to know. For example, [Give examples of each.]. However, in countries such as [example], where people's rights are
different from those in the States, the government controls the
news media and severely limits what can be broadcast or printed.
[Tell why; give examples.] The American government often cen-

sors information for national security reasons and not necessarily to infringe upon the public's right to know.

Sometimes, the American government censors information to protect national security. Since television and radio news is broadcast worldwide, people in the States as well as people overseas get up-to-the-minute reports on events, reports that used to take hours, even days, to receive. If everyone around the world has the opportunity to receive such reports, information the American government does not want known internationally, or even nationally, often is withheld — censored. [Give examples.]

The First Amendment to the Constitution of the United States of America lists freedom of the press as a right for citizens of this country. Freedom of the press allows certain liberties, but it is not an absolute. This freedom includes certain limitations, particularly in obtaining information. The president does have the constitutional power to withhold information deemed inappropriate or not in the interest of the people. So how does this limitation affect the citizens of this nation?

Most people are used to turning on the news on television or reading the newspaper to find out what is happening in this country and around the world. However, since the government imposes "gag rules" on the release of certain information, some information is not available to the general public. [Insert definition of gag rule.] Although the media provide a public service in their dispersal of information, some government sources limit the media's access to information other than information that is in the public interest.

What about the American people's right to know what is going on in the government? People in this country have a right to know what the government is doing, but do they have a right to know every single detail? Much of what the American government does, in both domestic and foreign affairs, is a matter of public record. Only in times of war or in matters of national security does the government have a constitutional right to withhold information from the people in this country.

What about how much information is censored here in the States compared to what is censored in other countries? [Give examples.]

Obviously, there are reasons for and against the issue of government censorship of news. People need to realize that what they hear and read is limited to a certain extent and that it may not include information that the government deems inappropriate to provide. People also need to understand that this limitation is not necessarily an infringement on as much as it is an enhancement of their rights as citizens of this country.

Once again, using questions her instructor provided, Maggie asked Miguel for some suggestions.

◪ A Classmate Responds

QUESTIONS FOR REVIEW

1. Does the draft seem to respond to the assignment given? Why or why not?
2. What is the main point of the draft? Can you identify the thesis?
3. What is your favorite part of the draft? What do you like most about that part?
4. What parts of the essay make you want to know more?
5. What suggestions do you have for improving the draft?

Miguel's responses to these questions were brief, but they were encouraging.

MIGUEL'S RESPONSES

1. Yes — it fits one of the choices we were given for the assignment. Your essay informs us about some aspect of censorship by showing a reason for government censorship.
2. The thesis is the last sentence in the first paragraph.
3. I still like the part about the Constitution. I like how you talk about what it actually says and what it implies and doesn't imply.
4. I want to know more about what we have a right to know and what the government doesn't want us to know. And what is a gag rule?

These answers gave Maggie some insight into how a reader reacts to an essay in progress and showed her that she was on the right track. She was ready to add the missing examples to her essay and finalize it for submission to her instructor. Maggie's final draft is reprinted at the end of chapter 4.

Chapter 4

Proofreading and Editing the Draft

4a   Proofreading

Proofreading — learning to identify errors — takes a lot of practice. You have to learn to read in a different way — not for content, which is the way you usually read, but for individual sentences or individual words. One way to proofread is to read your paper *backward, aloud, and slowly.* Begin with the *last sentence* in your essay and read it out loud slowly. If you read silently, you will read what you want to read — your mind will fill in any gaps that you may have in your writing. By reading aloud slowly, you force yourself to read exactly what you have written on the page. Does each sentence make sense on its own? Does it sound right? If you stumble at all in your reading, something is probably wrong with the sentence. This method of proofreading actually does not take very long and will help you find sentence structure problems. Trust your instincts — if what you read doesn't sound right, it probably isn't.

Now, how do you classify errors — and why should you? Unfortunately, there are no easy answers to the first part of that question. However, you can learn, with a little practice, to classify most errors. Some common errors fall into one of the following categories:

> subject-verb agreement (See section 6c.)
> pronoun-antecedent agreement (See section 6d.)
> spelling (See section 9g.)
> punctuation (See Part Four.)

4b

When you proofread your paper, try to put anything that doesn't sound right or look right into one of those categories. If the awkward structure doesn't fit one of those categories, check with your instructor for help in categorizing the error. Classifying errors makes you aware of repeated grammar problems to watch for in your writing. If you can find the correct category for a specific type of error, then you can use this grammar handbook to edit your errors.

4b   Editing

Editing means correcting errors. Because of recent advances in technology (word processors, for instance), we have become accustomed to something similar to error-free writing, but all of us still make mistakes when we write.

Obviously, your instructors will expect you to turn in a piece of writing as free from error as possible. If you follow the suggestions in this handbook for proofreading, identifying errors, and classifying errors, you can learn to make this part of your writing process somewhat easier.

The following example is an edited student paper with marginal suggestions from the instructor for identifying, classifying, and correcting errors. Study the instructor's suggestions as you read the draft.

Notice the indications of organizational errors, misspelled words, lack of agreement of nouns and pronouns, and incorrect verb forms and the suggestions for paragraph indenting and sentence revision. Once the writer makes these changes, the essay is in better shape, as the following draft illustrates.

Draft

Living in a ~~Foriegn~~ Country [sp]

[indent ¶] Many people will have a chance to live in or visit a ~~foriegn~~ [sp]
country at some~~time~~ in ~~thier~~ [sp] lives, either on business or [2 words]
for pleasure. For many people this prospect evokes both
excitement and anxiety. The thrill of living in another
culture, even temporarily, is balanced against a high level [reverse order to match ¶ organization]
of anxiety resulting from [not knowing the customs and not
speaking the language.] The experienced traveler eases her [s]

[change all pronouns to plural (non-sexist)] anxiety by researching the cultural habits of the country and
developing at least a working knowledge of the language of
the people they expect to meet.

[indent ¶] Knowing the language allows the traveler to do some [s]
basic things (he) takes for granted in (his) own country. For [make pronouns plural (non-sexist)]
instance, reading street signs and maps and using public
transportation requires a familiarity with the written
language. Asking for and understanding directions is much
easier if words can be used rather than pointed fingers and [change to active verbs]
other hand gestures. Without being able to read or write, a
visitor to an unfamiliar country could wander around for [s]
hours without having the slightest idea of where (he) (was) or [present tense]
how to get where (he) (needed) to go. Newspapers, of course, are [present tense] [make active]
written in the native language and are useful in finding a job
or a place to live. The traveler who needs housing should be
able to ask questions to find out whether electricity, garbage

Page Two

collection, and hot water are included in the rent. This

communication is not possible unless (he) speaks the

language. Using the phone, shopping for food and clothing,

and eating in restaurants can be difficult unless the visitor

knows at least some key phrases. Most importantly, making

friends is a lot easier if the traveler can speak the native

language. A friend can help by telling the traveler about the

customs and cultural habits of the country, which could

prevent some (embarassing) situations.

indent ¶ Knowing something about the cultural habits and customs of

the country helps the traveler understand the people and

their actions in a way that simply knowing the language

will not. For instance, in China saying "no" to a guest is

considered rude, so people often respond with "yes" even

when they (can't) honor the request being made. The unaware

change visitor (is) left wondering whether (he) (is) being ridiculed or

pronouns

to (was) not understood. In France (he) could be (embarassed)

plural

by showing up at someone's home even though they were

invited to visit at any time. To the French an invitation to

visit is just a polite thing to offer, rather like asking "How

are you?" in the United States. In some South American

Page Three

countries visitors should not admire objects in people's
homes for too long because the host would then be bound by
custom to give it to the guest. If the item was precious, the
guest would be considered rude and would certainly be
sp
embarassed. When someone offers a business card in Japan,
sp
the recipiant should look at it and comment on it. In the
United States businessmen and women simply pocket these
cards, which the Japanese consider rude. An employer would
not be pleased at the loss of business that might result!

indent # People who are lucky enough to spend time in a foriegn *sp*
country should make an effort to learn as much as possible
before traveling there. The more time that is spent preparing
to visit and learning the language and cultural habits, the
more enjoyable the stay will be.

*change as many passive
structures as possible*

Edited

Living in a Foreign Country

Many people will have a chance to live in or visit a foreign country at some time in their lives, either on business or for pleasure. For many people this prospect evokes both excitement and anxiety. Travelers balance the thrill of living in another culture, even temporarily, against a high level of anxiety resulting from not speaking the language and not knowing the customs. The experienced travelers ease their anxiety by developing at least a working knowledge of the language of the people they expect to meet and by researching the cultural habits of the country.

1 Thesis statement

1

Knowing the language allows travelers to do some basic things they take for granted in their own country. For instance, reading street signs and maps and using public transportation requires a familiarity with the written language. Asking for and understanding directions is much easier if travelers use words rather than pointed fingers and other hand gestures. Without the ability to read or write the language, visitors to an unfamiliar country could wander around for hours without having the slightest idea of where they are or how to get where they need to go. They need to know the language in order to read the local newspapers, which provide information on jobs and housing. The travelers who need housing should be able to ask questions to find out whether electricity, garbage collection, and hot water

2 First topic sentence relates to first point in thesis statement

2

3 Examples support and explain the topic sentence

3

Page Two

are included in the rent. This communication is not possible
unless they speak the language. Using the phone, shopping
for food and clothing, and eating in restaurants become
difficult unless the visitors know at least some key phrases.

4 Most importantly, making friends is a lot easier if travelers
can speak the native language. A friend can help by
explaining the customs and cultural habits of the country,
which could prevent some embarrassing situations.

5 Knowing something about the cultural habits and
customs of the country helps travelers understand the people
and their actions in a way that simply knowing the language
will not. For instance, in China saying "no" to a guest is
considered rude, so people often respond with "yes" even when
they cannot honor the request being made. The unaware
visitors are left wondering whether they are being ridiculed or
are not understood. In France travelers could be embarrassed
by showing up at someone's home even though they were
invited to visit at any time. To the French an invitation to visit
is just a polite thing to offer, rather like asking "How are you?"
in the United States. In some South American countries
visitors should not admire objects in people's homes for too
long because the host would then be bound by custom to give
it to the guests. If the item were precious, the guests would be
considered rude and would certainly be embarrassed. When

4
The most
important
example
is last, for
emphasis. It
also provides
a transition
to the next
paragraph.

5
Each
example
gives enough
information
about the
cultural
habit to
make its
relation to
the topic
sentence
clear.

Page Three

someone offers a business card in Japan, the recipient

should look at it and comment on it. In the United States

businessmen and women simply pocket these cards, which the

Japanese consider rude. An employer would not be pleased at

the loss of business that might result!

6

The conclusion summarizes the main points of the essay.

6   People who are lucky enough to spend time in a foreign

country should make an effort to learn as much as possible

before traveling there. The more time that is spent preparing

to visit and learning the language and cultural habits, the

more enjoyable the stay will be.

6

4c   Using the Word Processor

Writers who have access to a word processor have several advantages when it comes to revising and editing. With a word processor, once you type a draft of your writing, you can make major revisions without having to retype the entire draft. Word processors make moving and adding paragraphs, sentences, and words easy. Also, after you have a typed copy of the draft, you can more readily detect certain types of errors (like misspelled words, awkward sentence structures, capitalization problems) than you can in a handwritten draft. The main advantage to word processing is that you can revise (make text changes) and edit (correct errors) without having to retype or recopy the entire draft.

Other advantages to using a word processor include the following:

- You can store notes on a disk.
- With some practice you can learn to use a keyboard faster than you can use a pen, making it easier for you to keep up with your ideas.
- When you get stuck for ideas on a topic, you can turn down the brightness on the monitor and freewrite without seeing the words. This trick limits distractions and frees you to write ideas as quickly as you can generate them.
- You can use the "find" or "replace" commands to determine if you have either overused a particular word or misspelled it.
- You can use a Spellcheck program to pinpoint spelling errors and identify many typographical errors.

4d   Preparing the Final Copy

How do you know when the draft is finished? Once you have gone through the process of generating and rethinking your

4d

ideas, writing several drafts, proofreading, and editing, you will have a draft ready for recopying. Most of the time, however, you will have a deadline that pushes you through the writing process at a faster rate than you may appreciate.

When you feel comfortable with what you have written—or when the deadline approaches—you need to think about how you want the final copy, the finished product, to look. How should it be handwritten, typed, or printed from a word processor? Ask your instructor for specific instructions on format, or use the following suggestions.

HANDWRITTEN

1. Use 8½ × 11–inch college-ruled paper, preferably white.
2. Use black or blue ink (black usually preferred).
3. Leave 1- or 1½-inch margins on both left and right sides of the page.
4. Write neatly on every line (unless instructed to do otherwise) on only one side of the paper.
5. Number all the pages (in the top right-hand corner), with your last name to the left of the page number.
6. Put your name, instructor's name, course number, and date in the top left-hand corner of the first page.
7. Secure all pages with a paper clip.

TYPED

1. Use 8½ × 11–inch heavyweight paper (not onion skin or erasable).
2. Use a fresh black ribbon.
3. Leave 1- or 1½-inch margins on both left and right sides of the page.
4. Double-space everything.
5. Number all the pages (in the top right-hand corner), with your last name to the left of the page number.
6. Put your name, instructor's name, course number, and date in the top left-hand corner of the first page.
7. Secure all pages with a paper clip.

PRINTED BY WORD PROCESSOR

1. Use 8½ × 11–inch paper.
2. Use a fresh black ribbon.

3. Leave 1- or 1½-inch margins on both left and right sides of the page.
4. Double-space everything.
5. Number all the pages (in the top right-hand corner), with your last name to the left of the page number.
6. Put your name, instructor's name, course number, and date in the top left-hand corner of the first page.
7. Tear off the track feed, and separate pages.
8. Secure all pages with a paper clip.

4d

After you recopy, retype, or reprint your final draft, be sure to reread your essay at least one more time to look for words you may have omitted and typographical errors. If there are a few minor errors, neatly correct them in handwriting. If a page has many errors, however, you should retype or rewrite it to make it easy to read.

■ A Student Writes

Keeping in mind Miguel's suggestions for her revised draft, Maggie once again read her essay. As she went through each paragraph, she added examples to clarify or support her main ideas. In one place where she had asked a question, she could not think of any examples, so she simply deleted the question. She realized the question was not necessary and could be omitted without weakening the content of the essay.

After she added the missing examples, Maggie proofread her draft to look for possible errors. Then she followed her instructor's guidelines for essay format. Maggie was ready to submit her final draft to her instructor. Her final copy is reprinted on the next few pages.

Final Draft   MacGregor 1

Maggie MacGregor

Dr. Besser

English 1122

17 March 1993

Why Does the US Government Censor Information?

US government censorship of information involves

censoring official secrets that ensure national security,

which includes limiting the public's right to know about

foreign and domestic policies. In a democracy people usually

have a right to know what their government is doing in

domestic as well as foreign affairs. Sometimes, however, the

government needs to ensure that certain information does

not fall into the wrong hands. Differentiating between

government censorship of information and government

control of the news media helps to clarify the distinction

between what people need to know and what they have a

right to know. Government censorship of information is the

deliberate withholding of information for specific reasons

(usually national security), whereas government control of

the news media is dictating to the media what it will and

will not broadcast or print. However, in some countries in

Asia or Europe, where people's rights are different from

those in the States, the government controls the news media

and severely limits what can be broadcast or printed to protect leaders and to suppress truth. The American government often censors information for national security reasons and not necessarily to infringe upon the public's right to know.

Sometimes, the American government censors information to protect national security. Since television and radio news is broadcast worldwide, people in the States as well as people overseas get up-to-the-minute reports on events, reports that used to take hours, even days, to receive. If everyone around the world has the opportunity to receive such reports, information the American government does not want known internationally, or even nationally, often is withheld — censored. For example, during the Desert Storm situation information vital to the American effort was withheld from people in the States as well as people elsewhere. Strategies crucial to the military effort were classified by the government as not appropriate news.

The First Amendment to the Constitution of the United States of America lists freedom of the press as a right for citizens of this country. Freedom of the press allows certain liberties, but it is not an absolute. This freedom includes certain limitations, particularly in obtaining information. The president does have the constitutional power to withhold

MacGregor 3

information deemed inappropriate or not in the interest of the people. So how does this limitation affect the citizens of this nation?

Most people are used to turning on the news on television or reading the newspaper to find out what is happening in this country and around the world. However, since the government imposes "gag rules" on the release of certain information, some information is not available to the general public. A gag rule limits or restricts discussion or release of information to the public. Although the media provide a public service in their dispersal of information, some government sources limit the media's access to information other than information that is in the public interest.

What about the American people's right to know what is going on in the government? People in this country have a right to know what the government is doing, but do they have a right to know every single detail? Much of what the American government does, in both domestic and foreign affairs, is a matter of public record. Only in times of war or in matters of national security does the government have a constitutional right to withhold information from the people in this country.

Obviously, there are reasons for and against the issue of

government censorship of news. People need to realize that what they hear and read is limited to a certain extent and that it may not include information that the government deems inappropriate to provide. People also need to understand that this limitation is not necessarily an infringement on as much as it is an enhancement of their rights as citizens of this country.

Part 2

Paragraphs and Sentences

Part 2　Paragraphs and Sentences

Chapter 5

Writing Paragraphs

A **paragraph** is a group of sentences that explains one main idea. This main idea is stated in the topic sentence. All the other sentences in the paragraph explain the idea stated in the topic sentence. The length of a paragraph depends on how many sentences you need to explain the point you are making. The decision about how long your paragraph should be depends on how much information your audience needs to understand your main idea.

Readers can easily identify a paragraph by its indentation. In college writing the first sentence of each paragraph starts five spaces from the left margin (if you are typing) or about one inch from the margin (if you are writing by hand).

5a

5a The Topic Sentence

A **topic sentence** states the main idea of a paragraph. Usually, a topic sentence contains only one main idea that sets the context for the paragraph and presents the writer's attitude toward the main idea. One way to develop topic sentences is to take ideas from a brainstorming list and put them into sentence form. (See sections 1a-2 and 2b.) For example, if you are asked to write about the problems in the American health care system, you might generate a list of ideas in categories like the ones shown next.

CATEGORIES FOR HEALTH CARE ESSAY

Cost of Care

costly
need for good insurance
expensive hospitals

Medicare
cost of medicine
name-brand versus generic drugs

Horror Stories

sometimes don't hear horror stories
abuse of elderly

Quality of Care

some hospitals better than others
nursing homes
hospitals understaffed
nurses overworked

5a

Look at the ideas in each list (one list at a time) and decide whether one or more of the ideas can provide the basis for a topic sentence. Or look to see whether there is an implied link among the ideas. Using single or combined ideas, you can write topic sentences.

TOPIC SENTENCES

1. Most people know that health care is expensive, but they don't realize just how expensive it is until they are hospitalized.
2. People hear good things about health care but don't always hear the horror stories.
3. There are some problem areas in the health care system, like understaffing in hospitals.

Once you have a topic sentence, you can add examples and details for support.

DETAILS OR EXAMPLES

1. Give examples of prices charged for surgical procedures, hospital stays; explain where insurance money goes; give examples of cost of medicines.
2. Give examples of abuse and neglect.
3. Explain why the quality of hospitals varies, why hospitals are understaffed, why nurses are overworked.

Once you have considered all the ideas in your brainstorming list, you can use other invention strategies, such as interviewing and reading, to find further support for your topic sentence.

5b   Unity

Unity in a paragraph means that all the sentences in the paragraph support the topic sentence. The topic sentence should clearly state what the main point of the paragraph is, and the other sentences in the paragraph should offer specific details, examples, or facts to support that main idea. Notice how each of the following topic sentences sets the context of the paragraph it is in.

5b

EXAMPLE 1

Most people know that health care is expensive, but they don't realize just how expensive it is until they are hospitalized. [topic sentence] The average daily charge for a semiprivate hospital room is about $300, and most insurance policies will pay only 80% of that. If a person is in the hospital for one day, $60 may not sound like a lot to pay. Multiply that times three or four days, and the cost sounds worse. If the patient has surgery, add on 20% of the following: the cost of the operating room, the cost of the recovery room, the anesthesiologist's charges, the lab charges, the X-ray charges (if X rays were taken), the pathologist's charges, and the admitting doctor's charges. What starts out sounding like a minor expense can become an enormous one very quickly.

EXAMPLE 2

Magicians use their wit and their "gift of gab" as much as they do sleight of hand to present illusions. [topic sentence] Most of the time, magicians will talk and tell jokes in order to distract the audience. For example, magicians always say things like "there's nothing up my sleeve" or "notice the object in my left hand," just so the audience will look at the sleeve or at the left hand rather than where the sleight of hand is taking place or where a hidden object is located — such as in the right palm of the magician's hand. People in the audience are so busy listening to the magician talk or so busy looking for what is "hidden" that they miss the obvious. And that is how the illusion happens.

As in the examples, the topic sentence often is the first sentence in the paragraph.

5c   Development

A **well-developed paragraph** not only has a clear main idea but also presents enough information to convince the reader of what the writer is saying. For example, the following brief paragraphs illustrate a lack of development.

UNDEVELOPED PARAGRAPHS

I remember listening to music at Mass and listening to my father play the piano. He could play any song a person could hum for him. That was an incredible talent he had.

In elementary school I liked to listen to the rock-and-roll stations. In fact, I listened to them so much I decided to ask my parents to buy me a guitar. I wanted to take lessons, but they could not afford them.

In high school I practiced my music until I discovered I had some talent—not exactly the same talent as my father. I learned that I could actually write music. That was quite a revelation to me.

These paragraphs present an adequate discovery draft, but they do not have enough information to satisfy a reader. Once the writer adds some explanations and examples, the paragraphs become more informative and better developed.

DEVELOPED PARAGRAPHS

Music has always been a part of my life. My first memories of music are those involving people who I thought were great musicians. I remember as a child listening to the organ music at Mass, wondering if I would ever be able to play an instrument that well. I also remember listening to my father play the piano for hours at a time, envying his talent. He loved "taking requests" and could play any song a person could hum for him. He never had lessons; he simply had the ability to "play by ear."

While in elementary school, I listened to all of the popular music played on the radio—rock and roll, hard rock, and heavy metal—and decided that I wanted to learn how to play the guitar. After a lot of begging and pleading, I convinced my parents to buy me a guitar—a cheap one. Thus began my own real journey into the world of music. My parents could not afford to pay for lessons (for what seemed to them a whim on my part), so I experimented with sounds until I could pick out string combinations that sounded like music.

I continued my practicing throughout high school, and eventually I learned that I could do more than just play music. I could even write it. My parents were so pleased with my progress that they bought me an incredible-sounding acoustic guitar that I still have. Listening to music suddenly was more than just a pastime. In fact, it became the most cherished aspect of my life.

5d

The length of a paragraph usually depends on your audience, your purpose, and how much you want or need to say about the main idea. The length can also vary from a few sentences to many sentences, depending on the type of writing. For example, scholarly and academic writers often use paragraphs of great length; in contrast, journalists often use very short paragraphs.

5d Types of Organization

You can use practically any method you wish for organizing information in your paragraphs. You may use description, narration, definition, comparison and contrast, cause and effect, illustration and example, and classification, to name a few methods; or you may use any combination of them. These **patterns of invention**—or ways of thinking, which were referred to in Part One—can be used not only to generate ideas but also to structure them in paragraphs and in essays. Each method is defined and illustrated here.

A **descriptive paragraph** allows you to explain a perception about a person, place, thing, or idea. Vivid, concrete details and strong action verbs make a descriptive paragraph effective. Notice how the following paragraph uses vivid and concrete details like "huge feet" and "black or grey mask" to describe a particular breed of dog.

EXAMPLE: DESCRIPTION

Alaskan malamute puppies are quite a sight to behold. Usually several pounds at birth, they resemble massive balls of fur with four out-of-proportion, huge feet. The average malamute at six weeks weighs about 10–12 pounds — most of which is in the feet. Each pup has definite color contrasts, usually a combination of black and white or grey and white. The most distinctive feature, however, is the black or grey mask on the face surrounded by white on the muzzle and white and pink in the ears, which stand erect. The eyes are almond-shaped and are generally golden brown but very bright, reflecting the intelligence of the breed. The feature most people notice immediately after the face, however, is the size of the feet. Whoever said that a dog's foot size is an indicator of the full-growth size must have had a malamute for a pet. At full growth the once-cute fur ball becomes a huge 90–120-pound powerhouse sled puller — with even bigger feet.

5d

A **narrative paragraph** usually presents information in chronological order. Narrating is telling a story; and whenever events need to be related to the reader, chronological order helps keep the events clear and distinct from each other. Notice how the following paragraph uses a series of events to tell a story about a certain person.

EXAMPLE: NARRATION

As a young girl, I remember having several friends who would do almost anything for a laugh. For example, when I was about 10 years old, I met Cathy — crazy-as-a-loon Cathy who could make me laugh as no one else ever could. At lunch time she would put her milk straw into her nose and inhale milk from one of those little two-cent bottles that we bought. I remember laughing until I cried, or at least until the nuns scolded me. They never did scold Cathy, however. As I look back on situations like this, I often wonder how they kept from scolding her and how they kept from laughing hysterically.

A **definition paragraph** classifies or categorizes a word or an idea. It also gives the reader enough information to understand how that word or idea is different from other members of the same classification or category. The following paragraph, for instance, defines fiber by showing how it differs from fat.

EXAMPLE: DEFINITION

Fiber acts like a broom in your intestines, sweeping things along. Without it, waste gets blocked up, and the length of time your food takes to pass through your colon is greatly increased. This is particularly true if your diet contains animal fat because animal fats are solid at body temperature. They clog up your intestines just as grease clogs up drains.

—John Robbins, *Diet for a New America*

A **comparison-and-contrast paragraph** shows similarities and differences between two subjects. The following paragraph explains how two similar types of sled dogs differ in size and eye color.

5d

EXAMPLE: COMPARISON AND CONTRAST

The Alaskan malamute differs from the Siberian husky in several ways. The malamute is larger than the husky by twenty-five to fifty pounds on the average and usually has a smaller space between the ears, which are somewhat longer than those of the husky. The malamute has almond-shaped eyes that are generally golden brown rather than blue. Although both breeds are known as sled dogs, the malamute is a native American dog that was originally bred by the Inuit tribe of Eskimos.

A **cause-and-effect paragraph** can be organized in two ways. The paragraph can present the cause first and then discuss the effects, or it can show the effects first and then discuss the causes. The following paragraph explains the effect lost calcium has on the kidneys.

EXAMPLE: CAUSE AND EFFECT

The calcium lost from our bones due to excess protein has to go somewhere after it has served its purpose in our bloodstream. And so does the calcium we have ingested but have not been able to absorb due to high phosphorus/calcium ratios. It all ends up in our urine, producing very high levels of calcium in the kidney system, and all-too-often crystallizing into kidney stones. This is why kidney stones, the most painful of all medical emergencies, occur far more frequently in meat-eaters than in vegetarians.

—John Robbins, *Diet for a New America*

An **illustration** or **example paragraph** results from writers thinking "for example." An illustration or example shows or emphasizes what the writer says, and it also presents an idea (or ideas) for support. Notice how the following paragraph uses the example of a camel to illustrate the idea of aloofness.

EXAMPLE: ILLUSTRATION

We cannot help regarding a camel as aloof and unfriendly because it mimics, quite unwittingly and for other reasons, the "gesture of haughty rejection" common to so many human cultures. In this gesture, we raise our heads, placing our nose above our eyes. We then half-close our eyes and blow out through our nose — the "harumph" of the stereotyped upperclass Englishman or his well-trained servant.

—Stephen Jay Gould, *The Panda's Thumb*

5d

A **classification paragraph** presents categories into which the writer separates information. The following paragraph uses specific decades, such as the 1940s through the 1990s, to classify types of music.

EXAMPLE: CLASSIFICATION

At one time popular music was relatively easy to discuss in terms of "categories." During the 1940s most music was either big-band music, like that of Tommy Dorsey, or jazz, from singers like Billie Holliday. The 1950s, however, changed forever how people viewed musical scores. Suddenly, there were the rhythm and blues of Bo Diddley and the rock and roll of Elvis Presley. Then came the 1960s with the British-invasion music of the Beatles, the protest and folk music of Joan Baez and Bob Dylan, the bubble gum music of the Cowsills, the acid rock of Jimi Hendrix, and the endless rock and roll that led the way for the heavy-metal sounds of the 1970s and 1980s. Eventually, heavy metal made way for the punk and alternative music that became popular during the early 1990s. Now, when someone mentions a singing duo or group, like Shakespeare's Sister, most people find categorizing difficult. Is this a rock duo, an alternative duo, or simply two singers with a new sound?

5d-1 Arranging Details

When arranging details in a paragraph, you need to present your information in a logical order. A carefully structured paragraph enables your reader to follow your line of reasoning and better understand your intent. You can arrange details in a paragraph in several ways. The arrangement you choose depends on your purpose, the type of writing you are doing, and the commitment you make to the reader in the topic sentence. Four ways of arranging details are presented here.

Chronological order presents ideas either past to present or present to past. Notice how the following paragraph arranges details by presenting a series of events in the order of their occurrence.

EXAMPLE: CHRONOLOGICAL ORDER

5d

Once I got to high school, I realized that laughing aloud (or, rather, guffawing in a boisterous manner) was not always acceptable — at least not to the good holy sisters who were trying their best to make me into "a lady." I remember that one time when I was getting a stern lecture from Sister Karen Marie, I momentarily drifted off and did not respond to a question on cue. Sister became perturbed and yelled something like "Are you deaf?" to which my meek voice responded, "Pardon me, Sister?" I laughed so hard that I not only cried but also snorted — certainly not something "a lady" would do. I remember that Sister Karen Marie laughed also, although not as much as I did. And I also remember that while she laughed, she wrote out a detention slip for me.

Order of importance presents ideas either from least importance to greatest or from greatest importance to least. The following paragraph arranges ideas from the greatest importance, the creation of desires and habits, to the least importance, the development of new ads.

EXAMPLE: ORDER OF IMPORTANCE

One of the functional goals of national advertising is the creation of desires and habits. Major corporations spend billions of dollars each year on advertisements to arouse the desire in the consumer to try their products. Once the consumer tries the product and likes it, then the desire becomes habit. Thus, the individual is "hooked" into repetitive buying, which is one goal of marketing. Advertisers then continue developing a series of new ads to reinforce the buying habit.

Spatial order presents ideas that are usually descriptive. This type of arrangement begins with a focus on one point of reference, and then the description can go from left to right, forward to backward, distant to near, or top to bottom. Notice how the following paragraph presents details about a magician's load by describing it in each of these ways.

5d

EXAMPLE: SPATIAL ORDER

A magician's "load" is a device used to present the illusion of scores of feet of silk or paper streamers coming from inside the magician's hand. The load fits snugly inside the palm of the hand and is easily hidden. The load comes in several sizes but only one shape. It is shaped like a solid ¾-inch rubber band and is approximately 1 inch thick. The thickness is comprised of layers of material (silk or paper) folded and tightly layered in a criss-crossed fashion. This compact layering enables the magician to conceal the load easily. In the exact center of the load is the end of the material, pushed upward for easy access. The magician pulls from his hand what appears to be a small piece of material that in reality is a piece 50–60 feet in length.

5d-2 Other Paragraph Structures

Writers may choose any combination of the specific patterns just presented for organizing the information in their paragraphs. They may also use those patterns within the following three basic paragraph structures.

The **general-to-specific structure** presents very general information first and then focuses on specific details. Notice how the following paragraph begins with general information about two types of dogs and then ends with specific details about each breed.

EXAMPLE: GENERAL TO SPECIFIC

The Alaskan malamute differs from the Siberian husky in several ways. [general information] The malamute is larger than the husky by 25–50 pounds on the average and usually has a smaller space between the ears, which are somewhat longer than those of the husky. The malamute has almond-shaped eyes that are generally golden brown rather than blue. Although both breeds are known as sled dogs, the malamute is a native American dog originally bred by the Inuit tribe of Eskimos. [specific information]

The **question-answer paragraph** begins with a question and provides a possible answer. The following paragraph has a question and a series of examples for an answer.

Why do magicians talk so much when they perform? Most of the time, magicians use their "gift of gab" to distract the audience. For example, magicians always say things like "there's nothing up my sleeve" or "notice the object in my left hand," just so the audience will look at the sleeve or the left hand rather than where the sleight of hand is taking place or where a hidden object is located—such as in the right palm of the magician's hand. People in the audience are so busy listening to the magician talk that they miss the obvious.

The **problem-solution paragraph** states a specific problem and provides one or more solutions or explains why no solution exists. The following paragraph, for instance, organizes ideas by beginning with a specific problem and ending with possible solutions.

5e

EXAMPLE: PROBLEM-SOLUTION

Something needs to be done about the continued increase in health care costs in this country. [problem] The government can and should pass legislation that (1) limits the amount hospitals can charge for inpatient and outpatient services, (2) limits the inappropriate spending by Medicare and Medicaid, (3) limits the amount doctors can charge for services, and (4) eliminates insurance payments on "padded" invoices. [solutions]

5e Coherence

Coherent paragraphs have sentences that fit together logically. The ideas follow clearly and allow the reader to keep track of the ideas presented. Writers can make a paragraph coherent in the following four ways.

1. *Use transitions. (See the chart in section 3c.)*
Transitions give the reader clues about how the ideas in a paragraph fit together. The transition words in the following example are italicized.

EXAMPLE: TRANSITIONS

Political conventions bring out the best and the worst in people. *For example,* those people fascinated with political rhetoric will spend hours watching the speakers and listening to how each speaker uses the language. These same listeners will *also* gladly share with others what they have heard and what they have learned. *However,* those people who are bored with political rhetoric will more than likely ignore the speakers and, *instead,* spend hours complaining about the wasted time spent on television coverage of the conventions. Those people will *also* gladly share their complaints with others who may not be quite so willing to listen to the growls and grumbles.

5e

2. *Repeat key words.*
Repeating key words reminds readers that the sentences in a paragraph all relate to one main idea. Notice how repetition (italicized words) is used in the next example.

EXAMPLE: REPETITION OF KEY WORDS

The *Alaskan malamute* differs from the *Siberian husky* in several ways. The *malamute* is larger than the *husky* by 25–50 pounds on the average and usually has a smaller space between the ears, which are somewhat longer than those of the *husky.* The *malamute* has almond-shaped eyes that are generally golden brown rather than blue. Although both breeds are known as sled dogs, the *malamute* is a native American dog originally bred by the Inuit.

3. *Use parallel structures. (See also section 7d.)*
Using parallel structure—that is, keeping words or parts of sentences in the same grammatical form—makes the relationships among ideas clear. In the following paragraph the parallel structures are italicized.

EXAMPLE: PARALLEL STRUCTURES

At one time popular music was relatively easy to discuss in terms of "categories." During the 1940s most music was either big-band music, like that of Tommy Dorsey, or jazz, from singers like Billie Holliday. The 1950s, however, changed forever how people viewed musical scores. Suddenly, there were *the rhythm*

and blues of Bo Diddley and *the rock and roll of Elvis Presley.*
Then came the 1960s with *the British-invasion music of the Beatles,
the protest and folk music of Joan Baez and Bob Dylan, the bubble
gum music of the Cowsills, the acid rock of Jimi Hendrix,* and the
endless rock and roll that led the way for the heavy-metal sounds
of the 1970s and 1980s. Eventually, heavy metal made way for
the *punk* and *alternative* music that became popular during the
early 1990s. Now, when someone mentions a singing duo or
group, like Shakespeare's Sister, most people find categorizing
difficult. Is this a rock duo, an alternative duo, or simply two
singers with a new sound?

5e

The parallel structures in this paragraph may be
easier to see in list form.

the rhythm and blues	of	Bo Diddley
the rock and roll	of	Elvis Presley
the British-invasion music	of	the Beatles
the protest and folk music	of	Joan Baez and Bob Dylan
the bubble gum music	of	the Cowsills
the acid rock	of	Jimi Hendrix

Notice the pattern of parallelism: the type of music, the
word *of,* and the musicians who performed that type of
music.

4. *Use consistent pronouns.*

When you use pronouns consistently, you help
your reader keep track of who is doing what, and you do
not have to repeat the same words again and again. Notice the use of pronouns (italicized) in the next example.

EXAMPLE: CONSISTENT PRONOUNS

As a young girl, *I* remember having several friends who
would do almost anything for a laugh. For example, when *I* was
about 10 years old, *I* met Cathy — crazy-as-a-loon Cathy who
could make *me* laugh as no one else ever could. At lunch time
she would put *her* milk straw into *her* nose and inhale milk from
one of those little two-cent bottles that *we* bought. *I* remember
laughing until *I* cried, or at least until the nuns scolded *me. They*
never did scold Cathy, however. As *I* look back on situations like
this, *I* often wonder how *they* kept from scolding *her* and how
they kept from laughing hysterically.

To make sure that you do not confuse your readers, do not shift from *I* to *you* or from *they* to *you* unless your meaning demands this shift. (For a discussion on shifts, see section 7e.)

5e

Whole essays also benefit from the use of transitions, repetition of key words, and consistent use of pronouns. In addition, when writers exhaust their information on the main idea and want to change their focus — that is, go on to another main idea — they usually begin a new paragraph. Look at the deliberate change in focus in the following example.

EXAMPLE: CHANGING FOCUS

Before the days of newspapers and magazines, most advertising was mainly from shopkeeper's signs or town criers. The shopkeeper's signs were important to let the people know the shopkeeper's trade, because in these times businesses had no addresses, so their signs were the only way of advertising to the public. The town crier was the first means of supplementing sign advertising. Town criers were organized in a union and were accepted totally by the government.

Now advertisements appear everywhere around consumers. Ads from grocery and department stores appear weekly in local newspapers. Most people check and compare these ads before doing grocery shopping. The grocery ads not only contain certain sale items but also contain coupons, which help to draw in customers. "Buy one, get one free" is a gimmick advertisers use that helps advertise a product. After all, who can resist something free?

Notice that the first paragraph has a different main idea from the one in the second paragraph. The first paragraph addresses advertising before the days of newspapers and magazines, and the second discusses advertising today. Because of this new direction in thinking, the writer needs to begin a new paragraph.

Since readers need signals to guide them in their reading, you need to give them accurate signals. Whenever you change your focus and begin a new paragraph, signal the shift by indenting the first line of the paragraph five spaces. The indentation tells readers that you are shifting the focus and allows readers, at a glance, to make the transition needed for a clear and coherent reading of the text.

5f   Ending Paragraphs

Just as essays end with a concluding paragraph (see section 2b-5), a concluding statement will make your paragraph complete, or finished. This last sentence should reinforce your topic sentence but not necessarily repeat it. You can summarize your main idea, present a call to action, provide an insight, make a prediction, offer a solution to a problem, suggest an alternative, ask a question, or provide information that looks ahead to the next paragraph. All these approaches provide the reader with a sense of closure — a feeling that the written paragraph is cohesive and complete.

5f

■ A Student Writes

After several class discussions and in-class writings Tony Adam's instructor gave the class an assignment to write a paragraph on the topic of friendship. The instructor specified that the audience for the paragraph would be other members of the class and that the purpose would be to illustrate and give examples of friendship.

Tony decided to talk about his friend Bill. He began by freewriting about his friend.

FREEWRITING

Friendship means a lot to me. It means making people laugh, being there for someone who needs you, and not being afraid to tell your friend the truth. Bill was like that. He could always make me laugh. He was there for me, and he told me the truth — even when I didn't want to hear it. He made me laugh by doing silly things, and he was always available when I needed him. Bill was not an A student, but he was a nice guy. We went through a lot growing up together.

Tony thought that this initial writing had some good ideas, but it didn't make much sense. It sounded like he was saying the same thing several different ways. He decided to do some brain-storming to help him list and organize his ideas.

BRAINSTORMING

> Friendship is honest.
> truth
> support
> Friends like you when you don't like yourself.
> Real friends don't judge.
> Friends don't always take your side.
> Friends listen.
> Friends make you laugh.
> available
> share
> have time for you

Tony discovered that his list was rather vague and abstract and was missing concrete examples. He realized, however, that he could use some of these ideas in his topic sentence and then, for support, use concrete examples about his friend Bill. Tony also realized that he needed to get some feedback from a reader.

◪ A Classmate Responds

Tony wanted to know whether his thoughts about writing a topic sentence were reasonable. He asked a classmate, Rita, for some suggestions. After they worked together, they came up with a few more ideas for the brainstorming list and a possible topic sentence for the paragraph.

BRAINSTORMING

> trust
> comfort
> have your best interests at heart

POSSIBLE TOPIC SENTENCE

Friendship means trusting someone, making yourself available, and comforting another person.

These suggestions gave Tony some direction, but he still did not like the vagueness or the structure of the topic sentence. He decided to use a different approach to simplify the point he wanted to make.

REVISED TOPIC SENTENCE

A real friend is someone I can trust, someone who is available, and someone who is caring.

■ A Student Writes

Now Tony was ready to write a draft of his paragraph.

TONY'S FIRST DRAFT

A real friend is someone I can trust, someone who is available, and someone who is caring. As a young boy, I remember having a lot of playmates but only one real friend. Bill was my exact opposite. He was athletic, outgoing, and outrageously funny. We met as children when we lived in the same neighborhood, and we spent many hours playing together and dreaming up mischief. I remember that we were together so much that most people thought we were brothers. We went through elementary school and high school together, and I learned that Bill was one of the few people I could trust. He was always honest with me and told me the truth even when I didn't want to hear it. Whenever I needed him, Bill was available. One time while in high school, I thought I had met the "perfect girl." Bill was the only person who was honest enough to tell me I was wrong. I remember how angry I was at him—because I knew he was probably right. Even though he was not a great student, he worked hard. When my father died, Bill was there beside me, listening to me, comforting me, making me laugh, and letting me cry. I have never had another friend like Bill, and I doubt that I ever will.

Once Tony finished his draft, he asked Rita to read the new paragraph and give him some suggestions based on the questions the instructor provided.

◪ A Classmate Responds

QUESTIONS FOR PEER REVIEW

1. What is the topic sentence?
2. Are there any ideas in the paragraph that don't fit the main idea? Which ones?

Rita's answers to these questions gave Tony some helpful suggestions.

RITA'S RESPONSES

1. The topic sentence is the first one in the paragraph.
2. Sentences 3, 4, and 5 describe Bill, but they don't tell how he is someone you trust or how he is available or caring. The sentence about going through elementary and high school together says too much. The last part of the sentence about trust sounds good, but the first part doesn't really fit. Also, the sentence toward the end that says "he was not a great student" really doesn't fit. The rest of the paragraph sounds okay.

■ A Student Writes

After putting the paragraph draft aside for a day, and keeping Rita's suggestions in mind, Tony reread what he had written. Then he wrote another draft of the paragraph.

TONY'S SECOND DRAFT

A real friend is someone I can trust, someone who is available, and someone who is caring. As a young boy, I remember having a lot of playmates but only one real friend. Bill and I were together so much through elementary and high school that most people thought we were brothers. I learned that Bill was one of the few people I could trust. He was always honest with me and told me the truth even when I didn't want to hear it. One time while in high school, I thought I had met the "perfect girl." Bill was the only person who was honest enough to tell me I was wrong. I remember how angry I was at him because I knew he was probably right. Whenever I needed him, Bill was available. When my father died, Bill was there beside me, listening to me, comforting me, making me laugh, and letting me cry. I have never had another friend like Bill, and I doubt that I ever will.

Once again, Tony was ready to ask Rita if she would read his revised draft and answer some questions their instructor provided.

◪ A Classmate Responds

QUESTIONS FOR PEER REVIEW

1. Are there enough details to explain the main idea?
2. How are the details arranged (chronologically, by order of importance, question and answer, or the like)?
3. Are transitions clear?
4. What would improve the draft?

Rita's answers this time were more positive than before and gave Tony some insight into ways to improve his draft.

RITA'S RESPONSES

1. Yes, except a few more details about how Bill is caring could go before the last sentence.
2. The details are in chronological order. You could be more specific about when different things happened.
3. You obviously are impressed by Bill, but I'm not sure why you think he is so special. Tell us a little more about him — before the last sentence.

■ A Student Writes

Tony decided to add a few more details to his paragraph. His revised paragraph follows.

TONY'S THIRD DRAFT

A real friend is someone I can trust, someone who is available, and someone who is caring. As a young boy, I remember having a lot of playmates but only one real friend. Bill and I were together so much through elementary and high school that most people thought we were brothers. I learned that Bill was one of the few people I could trust. He was always honest with me and told me the truth even when I didn't want to hear it. One time while in high school, I thought I had met the "perfect girl." Bill was the only person who was honest enough to tell me I was wrong. I remember how angry I was at him because I knew that he was probably right. Whenever I needed him, Bill was available. When my father died several years later, Bill was there beside me, listening to me, comforting me, making me laugh, and letting me cry. I never felt like I thanked him enough for his friendship although I suspect he knew how I felt. When Bill died a few years ago, a void opened up inside me that no one has been able to fill. I doubt that I will ever have another friend like Bill.

Tony now felt ready to look at his sentences to see whether they were interesting and varied. The discussion of this next level of revision appears at the end of chapter 6.

Chapter 6

Writing Sentences

6a Sentence Form

A **sentence** is a word or group of words that expresses a complete thought. A sentence has a clear beginning (it starts with a capital letter) and a definite ending (it ends with a period, question mark, or exclamation point). A sentence has at least one independent clause — that is, it has a subject and a complete verb that together express a complete thought. A subject, which is often a noun or pronoun, is the person, place, object, or idea that the sentence is about. A complete verb expresses the action of the subject or the state of being of the subject. (For more information on complete verbs, see section 7a-4.)

6a-1 Simple Sentences

A **simple sentence** is one independent clause, which can have any number of words.

Yesterday afternoon, *Tom slipped* on an icy spot on the sidewalk. [*Tom* is the subject and *slipped* is the complete verb.]

The St. Louis Zoo is now *promoting* the conservation of endangered species. [*The St. Louis Zoo* is the subject, and *is promoting* is the complete verb.]

A simple sentence can have a compound subject.

Mary and her sister both *enjoy* ice skating. [*Mary and her sister* is the compound subject, and *enjoy* is the verb.]

A simple subject can have a compound verb.

> *She laughed and cried* during the emotion-filled movie. [*She* is
> the subject, and *laughed and cried* is the compound verb.]

A simple sentence can also be one word.

> Go! [*You* is the implied subject; *go* is the verb.]

> Help! [*You* is the implied subject; *help* is the verb.]

6a

Notice that some verbs express action (*slipped, is promoting*); others, called "linking verbs," express a state of being. This second kind of verb links the subject to a descriptive word (a modifier) or to another noun or pronoun that renames the subject.

> Those people *are* happy. [*People* is the subject, *are* is the linking
> verb, and *happy* is the modifier.]

> Nolan Ryan *is* a pitcher for the Texas Rangers. [*Pitcher* renames
> *Nolan Ryan.*]

For more information on linking verbs, see section 8c-2.

6a-2 Compound Sentences

Writers use compound sentences when they want to indicate that two related ideas are equally important. A **compound sentence** has two independent clauses (two simple sentences) connected with a comma and a coordinating conjunction; or with a semicolon, a conjunctive adverb, and a comma; or with a semicolon by itself.

> John became anxious about his date, and he decided to cancel it.
> [comma and conjunction]

> Sam feels tired, but he wants to keep on dancing. [comma and
> conjunction]

> Yesterday the temperature was 95 degrees; however, the humidity was lower than normal. [semicolon, conjunctive adverb, and
> comma]

Notice that a semicolon comes before the conjunctive adverb and a comma follows it.

> Mark decided to apply for a position as manager of a fast-food restaurant; his instructors' letters of recommendation helped him get that position. [semicolon]

For more information on conjunctions, see section 8f; for conjunctive adverbs, see section 8d-2a.

6a

6a-3 Complex Sentences

Writers use complex sentences to indicate that one idea is more important than another, related idea. A **complex sentence** has at least two clauses—one or more independent clauses and one or more dependent clauses. An **independent clause** has a subject and a complete verb that together express a complete thought. A **dependent clause** is a group of words that has a subject and a verb but cannot stand alone as a sentence. A dependent clause begins with one of the following words or phrases, called *subordinating conjunctions*.

SUBORDINATING CONJUNCTIONS

after	once	whenever
although	since	whereas
as long as	so that	which
because	that	while
before	though	who
even though	unless	whom
if	until	whose
in order that	when	

In a complex sentence, give the more important information in the independent clause and the less important information in the dependent clause.

In the following examples the dependent clauses are in italic.

> John was anxious about his date *although he was too scared to cancel it.*

0

Sam feels tired *whenever he works a long shift.*

Because of the number of dogs in his kennel, Jim decided to invest in dog food stock.

6a-4 Compound-Complex Sentences

0**6a**

Once you are comfortable using compound sentences and complex sentences, you may want to try combining several independent and dependent clauses into a more complicated structure. A **compound-complex sentence** has at least two independent clauses and at least one dependent clause. The dependent clause sometimes is a part of one of the independent clauses.

> Show the hockey coach how you guard the goal, and he will decide if you qualify for the team. [compound-complex sentence]

Notice the complicated structure of this sentence.

independent clause

Show the hockey coach how you guard the goal, and

dependent clause

independent clause

he will decide if you qualify for the team.

dependent clause

In this sentence each independent clause includes a dependent clause. Once these independent clauses are combined with a comma and the conjunction *and,* they form a complex-compound sentence.

Here is another example.

> Some food companies have decided to update labels on their products because new legislation on food packaging requires the change; these changes will benefit the consumer. [compound-complex sentence]

Notice the independent and dependent clauses of this sentence.

> Some food companies have decided to update labels on their products
>
> independent clause
>
> because new legislation on food packaging requires the change;
>
> dependent clause

independent clause

these changes will benefit the consumer.

In this sentence only the first independent clause contains a dependent clause. Once these independent clauses are combined with a semicolon, they form a complex-compound sentence.

6b   Sentence Variety

Writers strive to communicate information to their readers as clearly as possible. They also want to provide this information in a way that will motivate people to read what they have written. So writers usually vary their sentences to make them interesting to read. Suppose that the first part of this paragraph had been written in the following way.

> Writers strive to communicate information clearly. They also want to provide information. They want to motivate people to read. So writers vary their sentences. Then their sentences will be interesting to read.

Notice how dry, dull, and choppy these sentences are. They are all short, and they all start with the pattern subject-verb: *they want, writers vary*. The original paragraph has sentence variety and provides a better flow of ideas.

To make the sentences in a paragraph more varied—and therefore more interesting to your reader—you can combine sentences and move words, phrases, and clauses within sentences. How you vary your sentences will depend on which ideas you want to emphasize and how the sentences fit together as a whole.

6b

EXAMPLE 1

ORIGINAL: John was proud. He was excited. He had won the race. *(All are short sentences with the same pattern of subject-verb.)*

REVISION 1: John was proud *and* excited, *for* he had won the race. *(The first two sentences are combined using coordination; both ideas seem equally important. The third sentence is subordinated.)*

REVISION 2: *Proud and excited,* John had won the race. *(The modifiers are moved to the beginning. Because* proud *and* excited *come at the beginning of the sentence, they are emphasized.)*

EXAMPLE 2

ORIGINAL: Mary had one goal. This goal seemed impossible to achieve. *(The word* goal *is repeated unnecessarily.)*

REVISION: Mary had a goal *that* seemed impossible to achieve. *(The sentences are combined using subordination.* Mary had a goal *is emphasized because it is in the independent clause.)*

EXAMPLE 3

ORIGINAL: The dog moved around the house with her tail between her legs. She was ashamed that she had eaten the hamburger.

REVISION: *Ashamed that she had eaten the hamburger,* the dog moved around the house with her tail between her legs. *(The second sentence becomes a phrase that begins the combined sentence.)*

Using all short, simple sentences or a string of compound sentences can make your writing boring and difficult to read. Vary the patterns and lengths of sentences within a paragraph to keep your readers interested in what you have to say.

6c Subject-Verb Agreement

Writers need to make sure that the subject and verb of a sentence are either both singular or both plural — that is, the subject and verb must agree in number. This agreement is easiest to see when the verb immediately follows the subject.

> SINGULAR A *politician needs* to listen closely to his or her voters.

> PLURAL *Politicians need* to listen closely to their voters.

Identifying what should be singular and what should be plural is more difficult when the verb is separated from the noun.

> SINGULAR *Joseph,* John's lawyer and friend, *is* originally from Manitoba.

The subject is *Joseph,* not *lawyer and friend.*

Sometimes, a prepositional phrase between the subject and the verb is the confusing factor. The object of a preposition cannot be the subject of the sentence.

> PLURAL Obviously, the *ideas* of that person *need* to be recognized.

The subject of the sentence is *ideas,* not *person* (the object of the preposition *of*).

To identify the subject, look for who or what performs the action (or is acted upon); to identify the verb, look for the action performed by that subject (or on that subject).

6c-1 Subjects Joined by *and*

When the subject has two parts connected with *and,* the subject usually takes a plural verb.

A *computer* and a *printer are* useful tools for writers.

Joe's *talent* and his *ability* to charm people *make* him an ideal candidate for the job.

However, when the subjects joined by *and* refer to a single person, thing, or idea, the verb should be singular.

Eggs and bacon is my favorite meal.

When *each* or *every* comes before the parts of the subject, use a singular verb.

Each cat and *each dog wears* a tag with its owner's name.

6c

6c-2 Subjects Joined by *or* or *nor*

When the subject has two or more parts connected by the word *or* or the word *nor,* the verb should agree in number with the subject closest to it.

A typewriter or a *computer is* a good investment for a college student.

Good credit or two *cosigners are* necessary if you want a loan.

Neither my neighbors nor the *mail carrier likes* to come to my door when my dog is loose in the yard, even though she has never bitten anyone.

6c-3 Indefinite Pronouns as Subjects

When the subject is an indefinite pronoun, the verb can be either singular or plural, depending on the meaning of the pronoun. Use the following list to determine whether the pronoun is singular or plural.

SINGULAR	PLURAL
another	both
anybody	few
anyone	many
each	others
either	several

everybody
everyone
neither
no one
nothing
somebody
something

Each of the players *has* a separate locker.

Both of these women *are* excellent organizers.

6c

Some indefinite pronouns — including *all, any, more, most, none,* and *some* — are singular or plural depending on how they are used. If the pronoun refers to a noun that can be counted, that pronoun usually takes a plural verb. However, if the pronoun refers to a noun that cannot be counted, then the pronoun takes a singular verb.

All of the books *have* covers on them.

All of the stew *has* been eaten.

Some of the show dogs *are* beautifully groomed by their owners.

Some language *is* not appropriate for an audience of children.

6c-4 Collective Nouns as Subjects

When the subject is a collective noun that names a group (such as *committee, class, family, group*), the verb is usually singular.

The *committee makes* important decisions each month.

Brad's *family likes* all of his friends.

However, when the sentence emphasizes the individual members within the group, the verb is plural.

A *group* of people *were* discussing the latest tax increases.

Since the meaning is plural (a group cannot discuss, but individuals within the group can discuss), the verb is plural.

6d   Pronoun-Antecedent Agreement

A **pronoun** takes the place of or refers to a specific noun, which is called its **antecedent**. The pronoun and its antecedent must agree in number; they must either both be singular or both be plural.

> That *movie* won more awards than *it* deserved.

> Those *movies* won more awards than *they* deserved.

6d-1   Antecedents Joined by *and*

When singular antecedents are joined by *and,* use a plural pronoun when referring to them.

> *The dog and the cat* obviously didn't know *they* were expected to be natural enemies.

When *and* connects a singular and a plural antecedent, use a plural pronoun. To avoid an awkward-sounding sentence, put the singular antecedent first and the plural antecedent last.

> *The toddler and the preschoolers* can amuse *themselves* for hours with *their* kaleidoscopes.

6d-2   Antecedents Joined by *or* or *nor*

When singular antecedents are joined by *or* or *nor,* use a singular pronoun to refer to them.

> *Either John or Mark* will win the award for *his* performance.

> *Neither Rita nor Sally* wishes to break *her* bones while practicing the difficult sport of rollerblading.

When *or* or *nor* connects a singular and a plural antecedent, use a plural pronoun.

Neither Jack nor his sisters wished to visit the Yukon territory this year for *their* vacation.

6d-3 Indefinite Pronouns as Antecedents

When an indefinite pronoun is the antecedent, a singular pronoun is usually used to refer to it. Some examples of indefinite pronouns are *anybody, another,* and *everyone.* For more examples of singular and plural indefinite pronouns, see the list in section 6c-3.

6d

Each of the men wore *his* hair closely clipped.

When indefinite pronouns refer to people in general, avoid using masculine pronouns (*he, him, his*) to replace them. This use is considered sexist by many people. You can use *he or she, him or her,* and *his or her* to avoid sexist usage.

Everyone in class named *his or her* favorite songwriters.

Your writing can sound awkward if you use *he or she* too many times. Change the antecedent, the verb, and the pronoun to plurals if using the singular becomes awkward.

All my classmates named *their* favorite songwriters.

6d-4 Collective Nouns as Antecedents

When a collective noun is the antecedent, use a singular pronoun if you are referring to the group as a whole and a plural pronoun if you are referring to individual members of the group. Some examples of collective nouns are *class, team, committee,* and *family.*

The *class* voted to take *its* field trip to the National Archives in Washington, DC.

The *class* will pay for *their* own transportation to Washington.

■ A Student Writes

Tony's instructor decided to have the class review their paragraphs on friendship for sentence structure. The purpose of the assignment was to have students learn to use a variety of sentence types in their writing. The instructor provided the class with a list of questions to use for a review of each other's paragraphs. Tony asked Rita if she would review his paragraph for him.

TONY'S DRAFT

A real friend is someone I can trust, someone who is available, and someone who is caring. As a young boy, I remember having a lot of playmates but only one real friend. Bill and I were together so much through elementary and high school that most people thought we were brothers. I learned that Bill was one of the few people I could trust. He was always honest with me and told me the truth even when I didn't want to hear it. One time while in high school, I thought I had met the "perfect girl." Bill was the only person who was honest enough to tell me I was wrong. I remember how angry I was at him because I knew that he was probably right. Whenever I needed him, Bill was available. When my father died several years later, Bill was there beside me, listening to me, comforting me, making me laugh, and letting me cry. I never felt like I thanked him enough for his friendship although I suspect he knew how I felt. When Bill died a few years ago, a void opened up inside me that no one has been able to fill. I doubt that I will ever have another friend like Bill.

◪ A Classmate Responds

QUESTIONS FOR REVIEW

1. Does the paragraph have a variety of sentence types (simple, compound, complex, compound-complex)?
2. Do the sentences vary in length?
3. Do any of the sentences sound awkward?

Rita didn't have much to say about Tony's sentences.

RITA'S RESPONSES

1. You have used several different types of sentences.
2. You have some short ones and some long ones.
3. No, they sound okay.

Tony was pleased with Rita's responses. When he reread the draft, however, he decided to change a few things. He realized the fifth sentence seemed too lengthy for what he wanted to say. He changed it to read, "He always told me the truth even when I didn't want to hear it." He also realized that the sixth sentence would sound more precise if he told exactly when the incident occurred. He changed that sentence to "When we were sophomores in high school, I thought I had met the 'perfect girl.'"

Tony now believed his draft was quite good. He proofread the paragraph to look for errors and submitted it to his instructor.

Chapter 7

Common Sentence Errors

7a   Fragments

A **fragment** is part of a sentence — that is, a group of words that cannot stand alone — punctuated as though it were a complete sentence. Read the following paragraph and notice the flow of ideas.

EXAMPLE 1: FRAGMENTS

People use humor for many reasons. To communicate, to break the ice, to relieve tension, and to release emotions. And as a coping device. Because they don't know how else to react in a certain situation. Humor helps people cope with traumatic situations. Such as death, anger, or embarrassment. In fact, when people feel overwhelmed by their problems. Humor gives them a way to distance themselves and face the problems.

You probably think that this paragraph read smoothly. Now see what you think after you read the paragraph aloud slowly, beginning with the last sentence.

EXAMPLE 2: READ ALOUD

Humor gives them a way to distance themselves and face the problems.
In fact, when people feel overwhelmed by their problems.
Such as death, anger, or embarrassment.
Humor helps people cope with traumatic situations.
Because they don't know how else to react in a certain situation.
And as a coping device.

To communicate, to break the ice, to relieve tension, and to release emotions.
People use humor for many reasons.

Some of these statements are fragments. The fragments cannot stand alone and need a subject, a verb, or an independent clause to complete them. Let's examine methods for identifying these and other types of fragments.

7a

7a-1 Dependent-Clause Fragments

A **dependent-clause fragment** has a subject and a verb, but it begins with a word that signals that it does not express a complete thought. This word is called a **subordinating conjunction,** or dependent word. Here are some examples of subordinating conjunctions.

SUBORDINATING CONJUNCTIONS

after	even though	that	wherever
although	if	though	whether
as long as	in order that	unless	while
because	once	when	who
before	since	whenever	whom
even if	so that	where	whose

Now here is a dependent-clause fragment.

Because they don't know how else to react in a certain situation.

The word *because* signals that this clause is dependent.
To revise a dependent-clause fragment, either omit the dependent word that begins the clause or attach it to a related sentence.

People use humor as a coping device. They don't know how else to react in a certain situation. [subordinating conjunction omitted to make the clause independent]

Here is another revision.

> People use humor as a coping device *because they don't know how else to react in a certain situation.* [fragment attached to a complete sentence related in meaning]

The dependent clause can also be attached to the beginning of the sentence.

> *Because they don't know how else to react in a certain situation,* people use humor as a coping device. [fragment attached at the beginning of the sentence]

7a

Notice that when the dependent clause comes first, a comma follows it.

When you are revising, check each clause that begins with a subordinating conjunction to make sure it expresses a complete thought.

7a-2 Relative-Clause Fragments

A **relative-clause fragment** is a dependent clause beginning with *that, who, whose, whoever, which, whichever, what,* or *whatever* that is not attached to an independent clause. This type of fragment usually needs to be connected to the previous sentence to make it complete.

> He read an interesting article about the healing potential of laughter. [independent clause] *Which* gave some of the reasons all of us need to understand more about humor. [fragment]

Connect these two statements to eliminate the fragment.

> He read an interesting article about the healing potential of laughter, *which* gave some of the reasons all of us need to understand more about humor.

Here is another example.

> Sometimes, people use humor to distance themselves from tragedies. [independent clause] *That* they can't deal with otherwise. [fragment]

This relative clause does not make sense until it is added to the sentence (independent clause) that comes before it in the paragraph.

> Sometimes, people use humor to distance themselves from tragedies *that* they can't deal with otherwise.

7a-3   Phrase Fragments

A **phrase fragment** is a group of related words that lacks a subject and predicate but is punctuated as though it were a complete sentence. This type of fragment usually provides an example or illustration for an idea in a nearby sentence.

> Such as death, anger, or embarrassment. [phrase fragment]

This phrase can simply be added to the sentence that comes before it in the paragraph so that it makes sense.

> People use humor to cope with traumatic situations such as death, anger, or embarrassment.

7a-4   Verb Fragments

A **verb fragment** begins with a verb that cannot be the main verb in a sentence because it is not a complete verb. A verb fragment also lacks a subject.

One kind of verb fragment begins with the infinitive form of a verb (*to walk*). This fragment can be attached to another, related sentence; or a subject and a verb can be added to it.

> To communicate, to break the ice, to relieve tension, and to release emotions. [fragment]

This string of infinitives needs a subject and a verb to make it a sentence.

> *They* [refers to *people* in the first sentence of the paragraph] *can use* humor to communicate, to break the ice, to relieve tension, and to release emotions.

Another common verb fragment begins with the *-ing* form of a verb (*walking*). The *-ing* form cannot be the main verb of a sentence. It needs a helping verb — *is, was, were, have been,* and *had been,* for instance — before it to make it a complete verb.

> Learning that music can soothe and relax a person who is somewhat nervous. [fragment]

Two revisions are possible here. In both you begin with the question, "Who is doing the learning?" The answer will give you the subject of the sentence. For the first revision, add the subject and delete the *-ing* ending from the verb so that it can stand alone.

7a

> *People learn* that music can soothe and relax a person who is somewhat nervous.

The other possible revision is to add a subject and a helping verb in front of the *-ing* fragment. Adding the helping verb makes the verb complete.

> *People are* learn*ing* that music can soothe and relax a person who is somewhat nervous.

Now the sentence has a subject and the complete verb *are learning*.

Sometimes, a verb fragment begins with the phrase *being that*. To change the fragment into a sentence, omit *being that*.

> *Being that* animals have rights that some people refuse to acknowledge. [fragment]

The corrected fragment simply eliminates *Being that*.

> Animals have rights that some people refuse to acknowledge.

All the progressive and perfect verb tenses need helping verbs to make them complete verbs. To review these verb tenses, see section 8c-1a.

7a-5 Noun Fragments

A **noun fragment** is a noun or a group of nouns that can usually be attached to a nearby sentence.

> Malamutes are big dogs that enjoy chewing on just about anything. *Bones, rawhide, shoes, tables, chairs, fingers, and toes.* [noun fragment]

7a

Adding a colon between the two statements is one possible correction.

> Malamutes are big dogs that enjoy chewing on just about anything: bones, rawhide, shoes, tables, chairs, fingers, and toes.

Adding a subject and a verb to the beginning of the noun fragment list is another possible correction.

> Malamutes are big dogs that enjoy chewing on just about anything. *They like* bones, rawhide, shoes, tables, chairs, fingers, and toes.

Now let's look at a revision of the original paragraph on humor that began section 7a. The paragraph has been revised to eliminate the fragments.

> People use humor for many reasons. They can use humor to communicate, to break the ice, to relieve tension, and as a coping device because they don't know how else to react in a certain situation. Humor helps people cope with traumatic situations such as death, anger, or embarrassment. In fact, when people feel overwhelmed by their problems, humor gives them a way to distance themselves and face the problems.

See the difference?

You can avoid some of the fragment problems mentioned in these sections if you remember to ask yourself whether each word construction makes sense alone. Can the construction, when written on a separate piece of paper, stand alone? Or does it need something added to it so that it will make sense?

7a-6 Sentence Checklist

Use the following sentence checklist to help you find clause, phrase, verb, and noun fragments.

1. Does the construction have a complete verb (not just a verb with *to* or a verb with *-ing* but no helping verb such as *have, has,* or *had*)?
2. Does it have a subject (possibly an implied *you*)?
3. If it includes a dependent clause, is the clause connected to an independent clause?

If you answer "no" to any of these questions, you have a fragment that needs to be revised.

7b

7b Comma Splices and Fused Sentences

A **comma splice** is two sentences incorrectly connected with a comma. A **fused sentence** (or run-on sentence) has two sentences "run together" without correct punctuation and/or connecting words. The following sections give examples of comma splices and fused sentences and discuss the options for correcting them.

7b-1 Correcting with a Comma and a Coordinating Conjunction

You can use a comma and a coordinating conjunction to correct a comma splice or a fused sentence.

> COMMA SPLICE John was anxious about his date, he decided to cancel it.

> FUSED John was anxious about his date he decided to cancel it.

> CORRECTION John was anxious about his date, *and* he decided to cancel it. [add a comma and a coordinating conjunction]

7b-2 Correcting with a Semicolon

You can use a semicolon by itself or a semicolon and a transition word or phrase (see section 8d-2a for conjunctive adverbs) to correct a comma splice or a fused sentence.

CORRECTION

John was anxious about his date; he decided to cancel it. [add a semicolon]

John was anxious about his date; *therefore,* he decided to cancel it. [add a semicolon and a transition word]

Notice that a semicolon comes before the conjunctive adverb *therefore*, and a comma follows it.

7b-3 Correcting with Subordination

You can use a dependent word or phrase (see section 8f-3 for subordinating conjunctions) to correct a comma splice or a fused sentence.

John was anxious about his date *until* he decided to cancel it.

7b-4 Correcting by Creating Two Sentences

You can create two separate sentences to correct a comma splice or a fused sentence. End the first sentence with a period and begin the second sentence with a capital letter.

John was anxious about his date. He decided to cancel it.

7c Misplaced and Dangling Modifiers

7c-1 Misplaced Modifiers

A modifer—whether a word, a phrase, or a clause—should be placed as close as possible to the word or phrase it describes. Otherwise, readers may be confused about your meaning.

> MISPLACED MODIFIER The man was seen in the drugstore *on rollerblades*.

This sentence says that the drugstore is on rollerblades. To correct it, move *on rollerblades* to follow *man*.

> CORRECTED The man *on rollerblades* was seen in the drugstore.

The next example involves a misplaced phrase at the end of the sentence.

> MISPLACED MODIFIER The woman spent several hours in the library looking at books *with tinted glasses*.

This sentence says that the books have tinted glasses. To correct it, move *with tinted glasses* to follow *woman*.

> CORRECTED The woman *with tinted glasses* spent several hours in the library looking at books.

The following example also involves a misplaced phrase at the end of the sentence.

> MISPLACED MODIFIER Joan saw a car *walking to school*.

This sentence says that the car was walking to school. To correct it, move *walking to school* before *Joan* and add *While* to the phrase.

> CORRECTED *While walking to school*, Joan saw a car.

A modifier that is frequently misplaced is the word *only*. The following examples illustrate how the meaning of a sentence can change depending on the placement of the word *only*.

> *Only* yesterday, our team won the game. [indicates recent time]

> Yesterday, *only* our team won the game. [indicates our team alone]

> Yesterday, our *only* team won the game. [indicates that we have just one team]

> Yesterday, our team *only* won the game. [indicates that just our team won one game, or that winning a game was all that our team did]

> Yesterday, our team won the *only* game. [indicates that just one game was played]

7c

To make certain that a sentence clearly states your meaning, place the word *only* immediately before the word it modifies. Similarly, be sure to place the words *even, hardly,* and *just* immediately before the words they modify.

7c-2 Dangling Modifiers

Dangling modifiers do not clearly or logically refer to any word stated in the sentence. Usually, these modifiers are used as introductory statements that imply (but do not explicitly state) an agent of action.

> DANGLING MODIFIER *While giving the interviews,* the questions became clear to the audience.

This sentence suggests that the questions gave the interviews. If you ask, "Who gave the interviews?" you will find the subject that must be included in the modifier.

> CORRECTED *While Jim was giving the interviews,* his questions became clear to the audience.

The next example has a dangling modifier in the infinitive phrase that begins the sentence.

> DANGLING MODIFIER   *To end the season,* gifts were given to all the football players.

This sentence suggests that the gifts ended the season. Again, if you ask, "Who ended the season?" you will find the subject you need to add to the modifier. You may also need to revise the rest of the sentence, as shown in the corrected sentence.

> CORRECTED   *The coach ended the season* by giving gifts to all the football players.

7d

Remember to look at the placement of the adjective or adverb modifier and make sure that it modifies the correct word or words.

7d   Parallel Structure

Parallel structure refers to two or more ideas that are parallel in thought (or equal in importance) and that use the same grammatical structures. When presenting a list of ideas, be consistent and put single words with single words (all nouns or all adjectives), phrases with phrases, and clauses with clauses. The following examples illustrate some of these parallel forms.

> Readers interpret a piece of writing according to their *economic, social, political, religious,* and *intellectual* background. [all adjectives]

In this example each item in the list is a single adjective.

> Animals are not supposed *to be caged in a zoo* but are meant *to be free in the wild*. [all infinitive phrases]

Notice in this example that both phrases are structured in the same manner: infinitive phrase and prepositional phrase.

Another type of parallel structure is a list of words or ideas that have the same structure or are worded in the same way and are connected with a coordinating conjunction.

> Jack likes *boating, skiing,* and *ice-skating.* [all *-ing* forms of verbs]
>
> Jack likes *to boat, to ski,* and *to ice-skate.* [all infinitive forms of verbs]

Notice that the words and phrases in each sentence have the same form.

7d

SENTENCE 1	SENTENCE 2
boating	to boat
skiing	to ski
ice-skating	to ice-skate

One way to determine whether or not a sentence has parallel structure is to write down each item in the list and to look at the structures.

> Some days Sheila gets tired of driving to work, doesn't want to sit in traffic, or nervous about watching for pedestrians. [not parallel structure]

Notice that the phrases in this sentence do not have the same form.

> gets tired of driving to work
> doesn't want to sit in traffic
> nervous about watching for pedestrians

To make the structures parallel, change all three clauses to the same grammatical form.

gets tired	of	driving to	work
gets disgusted	with	sitting in	traffic
feels nervous	about	watching for	pedestrians

Now the sentence has a parallel form.

> Some days Sheila gets tired of driving to work, gets disgusted with sitting in traffic, or feels nervous about watching for pedestrians.

You can make constructions parallel by using **correlative conjunctions:** *either . . . or, neither . . . nor, not only . . . but also, whether . . . or.*

People who commute from rural areas to a city either *take a commuter train* or *drive a car* into town.

For exercise Neil likes neither *the treadmill* nor *the rowing machine*.

Yesterday was not only *hot* but also *humid*.

Parallel structure helps you to write clearly and effectively by maintaining a balance in your sentences and by maintaining a particular rhythm and pace. Notice the crisp, clear rhythm of the parallel structures in the following excerpt from John F. Kennedy's inaugural address.

7e

We dare not forget today that we are the heirs of that first revolution. Let the word go forth from this time and place, to friend and foe alike, that the torch has been passed to a new generation of Americans — born in this century, tempered by war, disciplined by a hard and bitter peace, proud of our ancient heritage — and unwilling to witness or permit the slow undoing of those human rights to which this Nation has always been committed, and to which we are committed today at home and around the world.

Let every nation know, whether it wishes us well or ill, that we shall pay any price, bear any burden, meet any hardship, support any friend, oppose any foe to assure the survival and the success of liberty.

7e Shifts in Tense, Person, and Number

A **shift in tense** refers to an inconsistent series of verb tenses within a sentence, paragraph, or essay. A change in tense is necessary only when you refer to events that occur at different times. The following examples illustrate tense shifts and their corrections.

SHIFT The author of the article *explained* the dangers of smoking. He *says* that nicotine and tar cause damage to the mouth and the nasal passages as well as to the lungs.

When referring to a piece of writing—that is, when discussing what an author says—always use the present tense.

> CORRECTION   The author of the article *explains* the dangers of smoking. He *says* that nicotine and tar cause damage to the mouth and the nasal passages as well as to the lungs.

7e

Verb tenses should be consistent within a sentence.

> SHIFT   He *went* home early because he *thinks* his mother *will need* help.

Since *went* is past tense, the other verbs must also be past tense.

> CORRECTION   He *went* home early because he *thought* his mother *would need* help.

A **shift in person** refers to the inconsistent use of pronouns. When using pronouns, don't shift from third person (*he, she, they*) to the second person (*you*) without a good reason. Also, make sure that *you* refers only to the reader. Otherwise, the reader will not have a clear understanding of who or what the pronoun indicates.

The following example illustrates these problems.

> SHIFT   The salesperson said that if *they* buy a new car, *you* can get better gas mileage.

Who gets the good gas mileage? Do *they* or do *you?* The shift in person causes confusion.

> CORRECTION   The salesperson said that if *they* buy a new car, *they* can get better gas mileage.

A **shift in number** indicates an inconsistent use of singular and plural verbs or pronouns. When using a singular subject in an independent clause, always use a singular verb and a singular pronoun.

> SHIFT   *A patient* in a nursing home *has* rights *they* sometimes *do* not understand.

CORRECTION *A patient* in a nursing home *has* rights *he or she* sometimes *does* not understand.

OR *Patients* in nursing homes *have* rights *they* sometimes *do* not understand.

The following example illustrates a common pronoun error that uses a plural pronoun to refer to a singular noun.

SHIFT Sometimes, a *person* will watch magic for so long that *they* will begin to see things that are not really there.

7e

Since *person* is singular, the correct pronoun is *he* or *she*.

CORRECTION Sometimes, a *person* will watch magic for so long that *he* or *she* will begin to see things that are not really there.

The other option is to change the singular *person* to the plural *people* and keep *they* as the plural pronoun.

CORRECTION Sometimes, *people* will watch magic for so long that *they* will begin to see things that are not really there.

Be consistent with singulars and plurals; do not mix them.

■ A Student Writes

For another in-class assignment Tony's instructor had the class review the first draft of a paragraph they had written for their classmates on the definition of junk food. The purpose of this in-class assignment was to look for fragments, comma errors, misplaced or dangling modifiers, and parallel-structure errors. The instructor had the students work in pairs and provided them with handouts of questions to answer. Tony had a draft that he thought was a good first draft, but he knew it needed some work.

TONY'S PARAGRAPH DRAFT

Junk food can be bought practically anywhere. In grocery stores, fast-food restaurants, gas stations, and vending machines. It is usually cheap and has no nutritional value. Some examples are potato chips, cookies, greasy burgers, fries, donuts, candy bars, and sodas. You eat this stuff and get a sugar or caffeine fix and then get sick. They should label this stuff better to let people know we're wasting our money. Instead of buying junk food, nutritional food should be bought.

Since Tony had worked with Rita before, he asked her to look over his paragraph draft and answer the questions on the instructor's handout.

◪ A Classmate Responds

QUESTIONS

1. Read the paragraph aloud, beginning with the last sentence first. Do any sentences sound incomplete? Which ones?
2. Are any sentences held together with commas rather than with periods or semicolons? Which ones?
3. Do any parts of sentences sound like they are misplaced or dangling? Which ones?
4. In each sentence, do the parts sound like they are not balanced or not parallel? Which ones?

Rita's answers to these questions helped Tony see areas in the paragraph that needed serious revision.

RITA'S RESPONSES

1. Something is missing in the second sentence. It sounds like a list.
2. No.
3. The last sentence doesn't really make sense. The second part of it doesn't fit with the first part.
4. In the second sentence *vending machines* doesn't match the other places. The third sentence sounds wrong.

■ A Student Writes

Tony decided to revise his paragraph, keeping Rita's suggestions in mind. He changed several sentences and tried to make his ideas clear and parallel.

TONY'S PARAGRAPH DRAFT

Junk food can be bought practically anywhere, including grocery stores, fast-food restaurants, and gas stations. It is usually cheap, maybe because it doesn't have any nutritional value. Some examples are potato chips, cookies, greasy burgers, fries, donuts, candy bars, and sodas. You eat this stuff and get a sugar or caffeine fix and then get sick. They should label this stuff better to let people know we're wasting our money. Instead of us buying junk food, nutritional food should be bought.

Tony felt that his paragraph still needed some work. The next level of his revision is discussed at the end of chapter 8.

Part 3

Sentence Parts

Part 3   Sentence Parts

Chapter 8

Identifying Sentence Parts

8a   Nouns

Once you understand how your sentences work, you can start looking at the individual parts of sentences to make sure your writing is accurate. The **subject** in a sentence tells who or what performs the action. The subject is often a **noun** — a word that names a specific person, place, thing, or idea. The **object** in a sentence tells who or what receives the action and is also often a noun. For example, consider the sentence "Sam wants money for his college tuition." The subject of the sentence is the proper noun *Sam;* the object is the noun *money.*

8b   Pronouns

Pronouns are words that take the place of or refer to nouns. Pronouns do not name a specific person, place, or thing. Instead, pronouns serve as a substitute for the noun so that the writer does not needlessly repeat words. A pronoun can indicate the subject of a sentence (subjective case), the object of a sentence (objective case), or possession (possessive case). There are many different types of pronouns, as illustrated in the following sections.

8b-1 Subjective and Personal Pronouns

A **subjective** or a **personal pronoun** is used as the subject of a sentence. These pronouns refer to specific persons, groups, or things.

	SINGULAR	PLURAL
First person	I	we
Second person	you	you
Third person	he, she, it	they

Sometimes, you may wish to use one or more of these pronouns as the subject of a sentence or as the subject in a second sentence that refers to a proper noun (or a specific group name) in the previous sentence.

I might find a way to finance a trip to Manitoba this year.

You could probably learn to play the violin with lessons and a lot of practice.

Larry thought that dogwood winter was a myth. *He* found out differently when it snowed on the first of May.

Who is also a pronoun that can be used as the subject in a sentence.

Who wants to know how to find the local zoo?

8b-2 Objective Pronouns

An **objective pronoun** is used as the object of a verb or as the object of a preposition.

	SINGULAR	PLURAL
First person	me	us
Second person	you	you
Third person	him, her, it	them

An objective pronoun can be a direct object (answers the question "what?") or an indirect object (answers the question "to or for whom?").

The postmark on the letter gave [to] *me* an indication that it had been in some kind of postal orbit for two months. [indirect object]

Whom is also a pronoun that can be used as an object in a sentence.

We owe our thanks to Brad, *whom* we honor today.

8b-3 Possessive Pronouns

A **possessive pronoun** indicates ownership.

	SINGULAR	PLURAL
First person	my, mine	our, ours
Second person	your, yours	your, yours
Third person	his, her or hers, its	their, theirs

Notice that possessive pronouns *do not* use *apostrophes*.
Possessive pronouns function as modifiers.

When Sally receives *her* award, she will put it on *her* mantel.

When Jeremy started *his* car, he discovered that *its* battery was drained.

Whose is also a possessive pronoun.

The officer would like to thank the man *whose* courageous act saved the drowning girl.

8b-4 Reflexive and Intensive Pronouns

A **reflexive pronoun** names a receiver of action that is the same as the performer of the action. An **intensive pronoun** emphasizes a noun or pronoun. Reflexive and intensive pronouns share the same forms, which are illustrated in the following chart.

	SINGULAR	PLURAL
First person	myself	ourselves
Second person	yourself	yourselves
Third person	himself, herself, itself, oneself	themselves

8b

These pronouns are often used incorrectly when either subjective or objective pronouns are the appropriate choices.

INCORRECT

Georgia and *myself* went to the movies.

Susie gave the ledger sheets to *myself* and my accountant.

Myself is used as a subject in the first sentence, so the correct pronoun is *I*. In the second sentence the objective *me* should replace *myself*.

CORRECT

Georgia and *I* went to the movies.

Susie gave the ledger sheets to *me* and my accountant.

The correct use of reflexive and intensive pronouns is shown in the following examples.

REFLEXIVE

Sarah gives insulin shots to *herself* each day. [*Herself* refers to *Sarah*, the subject.]

The finance committee agreed among *themselves* to increase the budget for part-time employees. [*Themselves* refers to *committee*, the subject.]

INTENSIVE

John Kennedy *himself* was the speaker at the ceremony. [*Himself* emphasizes *John Kennedy*.]

Nonstandard forms for these pronouns — *hisself, theirself, theirselves, themself* — are never correct.

8b-5 Relative Pronouns

A **relative pronoun** is used to introduce a subordinate clause.

RELATIVE PRONOUNS

that	whom
what	whomever
whatever	whose
who	which
whoever	whichever

A relative pronoun should be placed next to the noun (if there is one) it refers to in the sentence.

Terry was the *one who* decided not to watch the race.

When the team members left for the game, they forgot to get their *equipment, which* they left on the roof of the van.

She remembered to water the *flowers that* she had planted last week.

I do not remember *who* will be on call tonight at the hospital.

Some of these pronouns can also be used as demonstrative or interrogative pronouns (see sections 8b-7 and 8b-8).

8b

8b-6 Indefinite Pronouns

An **indefinite pronoun** refers to persons or things that are not specific.

SINGULAR	PLURAL
another	both
anybody	few
anyone	many
each	others
either	several
everybody	
everyone	
neither	
no one	
nothing	
somebody	
something	

The following indefinite pronouns are treated as singular pronouns.

Everyone in the neighborhood *is* outside enjoying the lovely spring weather.

However, *is anyone* brave enough to go swimming yet?

Some indefinite pronouns are singular or plural depending on their use: *all, any, more, most, none,* and *some.* (See section 6c-3.)

8b-7 Demonstrative Pronouns

8b

A **demonstrative pronoun** refers to a specific noun.

SINGULAR	PLURAL
this	these
that	those

Demonstrative pronouns must either refer to a specific noun within the sentence (*these buildings*) or must clearly refer to a noun in the previous sentence.

Linda thought about her *years* as a teenager. *Those* were wonderful years for her.

Those clearly refers to *years* in the first sentence.

This book doesn't have much of a plot.

This clearly refers to *book.*
Always make sure that demonstrative pronouns have a clear *antecedent* — a person, place, or thing the pronoun stands for or refers to.

8b-8 Interrogative Pronouns

An **interrogative pronoun** is used to introduce a question.

INTERROGATIVE PRONOUNS
who
whom
whose
which
what

Interrogative pronouns can be either singular or plural.

Who is that person? [singular]
Who are those people? [plural]

Whose book is on the table? [singular]
Whose books are on the table? [plural]

What is the time? [singular]
What are the answers? [plural]

8c

8c   Verbs

A **verb** is a word that shows action (*run*) or a state of being (*be*). All verbs have three principal parts: the **infinitive** (the word *to* followed by the verb: *to help, to ignore, to tire*); the **past-tense form** (*helped, ran, went*); and the **past-participle form** (the past-tense form with *have, has, had: have gone, has run, had helped*).

An **action verb** tells what a subject does.

John *canceled* his date.
My dog *had* a litter of eight puppies yesterday.
Sam *watches* television during the day.
Those people *will listen* to the concert on the radio.

A verb can also show the existence of a person, place, thing, or idea (*to be, to appear, to seem, to become*). (See section 8c-2 on linking verbs.)

Susie *is* a very sweet girl.
That sky *appears* threatening.
Does he *seem* weird, or *is* it just my imagination?
Those pilots *became* expert fliers very quickly.

8c-1 Tenses

8c-1a Regular Verbs

Verbs express action or states of being according to time — the present, the past, or the future. Verb tenses are different forms of the verb used to represent action or existence at different times. To form the tenses of regular verbs, follow these rules.

PRESENT TENSE The present tense expresses action occurring now (present verb form).

	SINGULAR	PLURAL
First person	I help	we help
Second person	you help	you help
Third person	he, she, it helps	they help

Notice that only the third-person singular form of the present-tense verb has an *-s* ending.

PAST TENSE The past tense expresses completed past action (present verb form + *-d* or + *-ed*).

	SINGULAR	PLURAL
First person	I helped	we helped
Second person	you helped	you helped
Third person	he, she, it helped	they helped

FUTURE TENSE The future tense expresses action that will happen (*will* + present verb form).

	SINGULAR	PLURAL
First person	I will help	we will help
Second person	you will help	you will help
Third person	he, she, it will help	they will help

All regular verbs have perfect tenses that use *have, has,* or *had* plus the past-tense form of the verb. These verb forms express action in the following ways.

PRESENT PERFECT The present perfect tense expresses past

8c

action that continues into the present (*have* or *has* + the -*d* or
-*ed* form).

	SINGULAR	PLURAL
First person	I have helped	we have helped
Second person	you have helped	you have helped
Third person	he, she, it has helped	they have helped

The present perfect tense indicates action that started in
the past and continues in the present.

Lawrence *has studied* French for ten years.

This tense can also indicate an action that was completed at an
unspecified time in the past.

8c

John *has helped* his parents move from one house to another
many times.

PAST PERFECT The past perfect tense expresses completed
past action that happened before another past action (*had* + the
-*d* or -*ed* form).

	SINGULAR	PLURAL
First person	I had helped	we had helped
Second person	you had helped	you had helped
Third person	he, she, it had helped	they had helped

The past perfect tense indicates past action in a chronological sequence so that it is clear which past action happened first.

Once he *had heard* about his friends' fears, Tommy offered to
stay with them. (First he heard about their fears; then he offered
to stay with them.)

FUTURE PERFECT The future perfect tense expresses action that will be completed by a certain time (*will have* + the -*d*
or -*ed* form).

	SINGULAR	PLURAL
First person	I will have helped	we will have helped
Second person	you will have helped	you will have helped
Third person	he, she, it will have helped	they will have helped

The future perfect tense indicates action that will be completed by a specified time in the future.

Tony *will have returned* from Scotland by the time summer gets here.

Progressive verbs indicate action that continues over a period of time. This verb form is also known as the *continuous form* of the verb; it can be used in the present, past, or future tense.

PRESENT PROGRESSIVE The present progressive form expresses current continuous action (*am, is, are* + present verb form + *-ing*).

	SINGULAR	PLURAL
First person	I am helping	we are helping
Second person	you are helping	you are helping
Third person	he, she, it is helping	they are helping

PAST PROGRESSIVE The past progressive form expresses continuous past action (*was, were* + present verb form + *-ing*).

	SINGULAR	PLURAL
First person	I was helping	we were helping
Second person	you were helping	you were helping
Third person	he, she, it was helping	they were helping

FUTURE PROGRESSIVE The future progressive form expresses continuous future action (*will be* + present verb form + *-ing*).

	SINGULAR	PLURAL
First person	I will be helping	we will be helping
Second person	you will be helping	you will be helping
Third person	he, she, it will be helping	they will be helping

The progressive form is not a verb tense and does not show time. It is used to indicate continuous action within a certain time. It must be used with a helping verb like *is, am, are, was, were,* or *will be.*

8c-1b Irregular Verbs

Many verbs do not follow the rules for regular verbs. These verbs are called **irregular verbs** because they have past-tense forms and past-participle forms that do not follow the regular-verb patterns. The following list gives the forms for selected irregular verbs.

SOME COMMON IRREGULAR VERBS

Present	*Past*	*Past Participle*
arise	arose	arisen
awake	awoke	awaked
be	was/were	been
bear (to carry)	bore	borne
bear (to give birth)	bore	borne, born
beat	beat	beaten, beat
become	became	become
begin	began	begun
bend	bent	bent
bet	bet	bet
bite	bit	bitten, bit
bleed	bled	bled
blow	blew	blown
break	broke	broken
bring	brought	brought
build	built	built
burst	burst	burst
buy	bought	bought
catch	caught	caught

Present	*Past*	*Past Participle*
choose	chose	chosen
cling	clung	clung
come	came	come
cost	cost	cost
creep	crept	crept
cut	cut	cut
deal	dealt	dealt
dig	dug	dug
dive	dived, dove	dived
do	did	done
drag	dragged	dragged
draw	drew	drawn
dream	dreamed, dreamt	dreamed, dreamt
drink	drank	drunk
drive	drove	driven
drown	drowned	drowned
eat	ate	eaten
fall	fell	fallen
feed	fed	fed
feel	felt	felt
fight	fought	fought
find	found	found
fly	flew	flown
forget	forgot	forgotten
freeze	froze	frozen
get	got	gotten, got
give	gave	given
go	went	gone
grow	grew	grown
hang (to suspend an object)	hung	hung
hang (to kill a person)	hanged	hanged
have	had	had
hear	heard	heard
hide	hid	hidden
hit	hit	hit
hold	held	held
hurt	hurt	hurt

8c

Present	*Past*	*Past Participle*
keep	kept	kept
know	knew	known
lay (to put, to place)	laid	laid
lead	led	led
lend	lent	lent
let	let	let
lie (to recline)	lay	lain
light	lighted, lit	lighted, lit
lose	lost	lost
make	made	made
mean	meant	meant
meet	met	met
pay	paid	paid
prove	proved	proved, proven
put	put	put
quit	quit	quit
read	read	read
ride	rode	ridden
ring	rang	rung
rise	rose	risen
run	ran	run
say	said	said
see	saw	seen
sell	sold	sold
send	sent	sent
set	set	set
sew	sewed	sewed, sewn
shake	shook	shaken
shave	shaved	shaved, shaven
shine	shone	shone
shoot	shot	shot
show	showed	shown
shrink	shrank	shrunk
shut	shut	shut
sing	sang	sung
sink	sank	sunk
sit	sat	sat
slay	slew	slain
sleep	slept	slept
slide	slid	slid, slidden

8c

Present	*Past*	*Past Participle*
speak	spoke	spoken
speed	sped	sped
spend	spent	spent
spin	spun	spun
spring	sprang	sprung
stand	stood	stood
steal	stole	stolen
stick	stuck	stuck
sting	stung	stung
strike	struck	struck
swear	swore	sworn
sweep	swept	swept
swim	swam	swum
swing	swung	swung
take	took	taken
teach	taught	taught
tear	tore	torn
tell	told	told
think	thought	thought
throw	threw	thrown
wake	waked, woke	waked, woken
wear	wore	worn
weave	wove	woven
weep	wept	wept
win	won	won
wind	wound	wound
wring	wrung	wrung
write	wrote	written

8c

8c-2 Linking Verbs

Linking verbs do not state action. Instead, they express a state of being. They link a subject to a word that describes the subject or to a word that renames the subject. Common linking verbs are *to be* (including the forms *is, am, are, was, were, be, been, being*), *to become* (*become, becomes, becoming, became*), *to feel, to seem, to appear,* and *to look.*

The following examples show how linking verbs can be used to connect a subject to a word that describes it.

John *became* anxious about his date for the play. [*John* is the subject; *anxious* describes *John*.]

Sam *feels* as though he needs to change jobs.

This book *seems* heavy compared with the others.

The next examples show linking verbs that connect a subject to a word that renames it.

Tom and Carol *remained* good friends. [*Tom and Carol* is the subject; *good friends* renames *Tom and Carol*.]

Marilyn *is* a wonderful mother.

The buffalo *were* prairie animals.

8c-3 Voice

8c

The **voice** of a verb tells whether the subject performs action or is acted upon. In the **active voice** the subject performs the action.

John canceled his date.

The *dog chews* its toy.

I will give you directions to the city.

In the **passive voice** either the subject is acted upon or the performer of the action is unknown. The passive voice uses a form of the verb *to be* (*is, am, are, was, were, be, been, being*) plus the past-participle form.

Taxes *were increased* this year. [The subject is acted upon.]

The door *had been broken* into several pieces. [The performer of the action is unknown.]

Form the passive by using the following rules.

PRESENT PASSIVE Use a present form of *to be* plus the past participle.

When I go to the market, I *am helped* immediately.

PAST PASSIVE Use a past-tense form of *to be* plus the past participle.

They *were handed* their boarding passes as soon as they bought their tickets.

FUTURE PASSIVE Use *will be* plus the past participle.

Sandy has decided that she *will be heard* at the next political rally.

PRESENT PERFECT PASSIVE Use *have been* or *has been* plus the past participle.

You *have been treated* graciously during your vacations in the Yukon.

PAST PERFECT PASSIVE Use *had been* plus the past participle.

Johnson *had been given* time to retreat, but he decided to stay.

FUTURE PERFECT PASSIVE Use *will have been* plus the past participle.

The new plans *will have been finished* by this time tomorrow.

You should use the active voice as much as possible to eliminate wordiness and to make your writing clear and direct. The following two paragraphs illustrate how much clearer the active voice is than the passive voice.

PASSIVE VOICE

Millions of dollars *are spent* each year on advertisements to arouse consumer desire. Once the advertised product *is tried* by the consumer, the desire *is turned* into habit. Then the individual *is hooked* into repetitive buying.

ACTIVE VOICE

Advertisers *spend* millions of dollars each year to arouse consumer desire. Once consumers *try* the advertised product, the desire *turns* into habit. Then repetitive buying *hooks* the consumer.

The italicized passive-voice structures in the first example blur the impact of the writer's ideas about advertising. In contrast, the active-voice structures in the second example clarify those ideas.

However, not all passive verbs can or should be changed into active verbs. Sometimes, the performer of the action is not known; sometimes, the receiver of the action is more important than the performer of the action; and sometimes, the passive voice is a customary structure.

> State and local taxes were raised again this year. [performer unknown]
>
> The flight from Kansas City to Chicago has been delayed because of snow. [receiver important]
>
> Shoplifters are prosecuted. [customary usage]

8d

8d Adjectives, Adverbs, and Articles

8d-1 Adjectives

An **adjective** describes (modifies) a noun or, in a few cases, a pronoun. Notice how the adjectives modify the nouns in the following examples.

> Without humor this world would be full of *solemn, glum* people.
>
> *Some* ads make promises that are hard to believe.
>
> *Those rain* clouds appeared quickly.

The next sentence shows an adjective that modifies a pronoun.

> The Cadillac was a *new* one.

8d-2 Adverbs

An **adverb** modifies a verb, an adjective, or another adverb. Some adverbs are formed by adding *-ly* to an adjective.

soft, soft*ly*   loud, loud*ly*
smooth, smooth*ly*   slow, slow*ly*
heavy, heavi*ly*   weak, weak*ly*

Generally, an adverb answers the questions *when, where, why, how, how often,* or *to what extent*. Notice how the adverbs answer questions in the following examples. Also notice the words the adverbs modify.

8d

The paper came *yesterday*. [came *when?*]

I found my glasses *here* on the table. [found my glasses *where?*]

Those shoes fit her *perfectly*. [fit *how?*]

Police officers have to be *extremely* cautious. [cautious *to what extent?*]

Place an adverb as close as possible to the word or phrase it modifies so that the reader can clearly understand what you have written.

8d-2a Conjunctive Adverbs

A **conjunctive adverb** sometimes connects clauses in compound sentences. Some conjunctive adverbs are *accordingly, consequently, furthermore, however, moreover, nevertheless, therefore*. When a conjunctive adverb connects two independent clauses, use a semicolon before the adverb and a comma after it.

Snow is typical during January in the northern states; *however,* 20 inches is still considered to be a record amount.

Whenever she notices other employees leaving work early, she wonders if she should too; *nevertheless,* she stays and finishes her job.

8d-2b Incorrect Adverb Forms

Avoid the following adverbs, which indicate double negatives.

INCORRECT	CORRECT
can't hardly	can hardly
not any	not one, none
can't barely	can barely

8d-3 Comparatives and Superlatives

8d-3a Comparatives

You can also use adjectives and adverbs for comparisons. The **comparative form** is used to compare *two* persons, places, objects, ideas, or actions. The comparative form uses one of three possible structures. It may add -*er* to the modifier for most one- or two-syllable modifiers. It may use the word *more* with the modifier for most modifiers that have three or more syllables. Or it may use the word *less* with the modifier.

> Your stray cat is *friendlier* than my Siamese.

> Susan's ideas have provided *more imaginative* alternatives for the company's hiring practices.

> The sky is *less cloudy* today than it was yesterday.

Do not use both the word *more* and the -*er* ending at the same time (*friendlier* or *more friendly,* not *more friendlier*). For some modifiers of three syllables or more, do not use the -*er* ending at all.

more courteous	*not* courteouser
more elegant	*not* eleganter
more excited	*not* exciteder

8d-3b Superlatives

To compare *three or more* persons, places, objects, ideas, or actions, use the **superlative form**. The superlative form adds -*est* to the modifier, uses the word *most* with the modifier, or uses the word *least* with it.

> Your cat is the *friendliest* one I know.

> The sky is the *bluest* it has been all week.

8d

Her ideas for expansion are the *least productive* we have seen this year.

Some movies present the *most bizarre* perspectives on romance imaginable.

Do not use both the *-est* ending and the word *most* at the same time. For some modifiers of three syllables or more, do not use the *-est* ending at all.

most courteous	*not* courteousest
most elegant	*not* elegantest
most excited	*not* excitedest

Note that some adjectives and adverbs have irregular forms.

8d

bad	worse	worst
badly	worse	worst
good	better	best
little	less	least
many	more	most
well	better	best

8d-4 Articles

An **article** is a word (usually classified as a type of adjective) used to mark nouns as either general (*a, an*) or specific (*the*).

A horse can give you some enjoyment.

John read *the* last novel that Mark Twain wrote.

The sky has beautiful clouds.

An orange tastes great in *the* morning.

Use *a* before a word that begins with a consonant sound (*b, c, d, f, g, h, j, k, l, m, n, p, q, r, s, t, v, w, x, y, z*). Use *an* before a word that begins with a vowel sound (*a, e, i, o, u,* and sometimes *h*). *A* and *an* describe general nouns: *a* book, *an* apple, *a* town. *The* describes specific nouns: *the* book, *the* apple, *the* town.

Often, an idiomatic structure determines the use or omission of an article.

I went to college. [idiomatic; no article necessary.]

I went to *a* university. [general]

I went to *the* university. [a specific one]

8e Prepositions

A **preposition** is a word used to connect a noun or a pronoun to another part of the sentence. When writers use a preposition to create a modifier, they produce a prepositional phrase. A **prepositional phrase** includes a preposition, its object, and any modifiers of that object.

Someone I've never seen before is *in the house*.

The prepositional phrase *in the house* describes the location of *someone*. The preposition is *in*, its object is *house*, and *the* modifies *house*.

A sentence can have more than one prepositional phrase.

"Somewhere *Over the Rainbow*" is one *of the greatest songs* Judy Garland ever sang.

The prepositional phrase *Over the Rainbow* describes *Somewhere*, and *of the greatest songs* describes one.

Prepositions express many different kinds of relationships between words. The following list gives some common prepositions.

about	among	below
above	around	beside
across	as	between
after	at	beyond
against	before	by
along	behind	down

during	off	to
for	on	toward
from	onto	under
in	out	underneath
inside	outside	until
into	over	upon
near	through	with
next	throughout	without
of		

8f   Conjunctions

8f

Conjunctions are words used to join parts of a sentence. You can also use conjunctions to join words, phrases, and clauses. There are three different types of conjunctions: coordinating, correlative, and subordinating.

8f-1   Coordinating Conjunctions

Coordinating conjunctions (*and, but, or, nor, for, so, yet*) connect only equal grammatical structures. Use coordinating conjunctions to link words, phrases, or clauses of equal importance.

People who like the outdoors often like hiking, camping, *and* boating. [connects words]

You can find humor in the workplace, in the home, *and* in the media. [connects phrases]

Horses are nice pets to have, *but* they need a lot of exercise. [connects clauses]

8f-2   Correlative Conjunctions

Correlative conjunctions (*either . . . or, neither . . . nor, not only . . . but also, both . . . and, whether . . . or*) also connect only equal grammatical structures. Use these conjunctions to link words, phrases, or clauses that have equal importance.

Yesterday was *not only* hot *but also* humid. [connects words]

The local transit system offers low fares to *both* students on financial aid *and* senior citizens on a fixed income. [connects phrases]

Either the school will be closed because of this snowstorm *or* it will not. [connects clauses]

8f-3 Subordinating Conjunctions

A **subordinating conjunction** introduces a dependent clause. The dependent clause in a sentence carries less important information than the independent clause. The dependent clause may follow or precede the independent clause.

8f

The zoo will not remain open on Sundays *unless* more people donate money during the annual fund-raising campaign. [dependent clause last]

Unless more people donate money during the annual fund-raising campaign, the zoo will not remain open on Sundays. [dependent clause first]

Sled dogs enjoy winter weather *although* some other dogs cannot tolerate the cold. [dependent clause last]

Although some other dogs cannot tolerate the cold, sled dogs enjoy winter weather. [dependent clause first]

Notice that when the dependent clause comes first, it is separated from the independent clause by a comma. No comma is needed when the independent clause comes first.

The following list gives some common subordinating conjunctions.

SUBORDINATING CONJUNCTIONS

after	as long as	if
although	because	in order that
as	before	once
as if	even though	rather than

since	unless	where
so that	until	whereas
than	when	whether
that	whenever	while
though		

8g Interjections

An **interjection** expresses surprise or emotion. These words can be used alone or as part of a sentence.

Oops!

Well, that is a sad situation.

Wow! John just had the winning goal.

An exclamation point is used only when strong emotion is expressed. If the interjection expresses mild emotion, use a comma after it to separate it from the rest of the sentence.

■ A Student Writes

After several class discussions about levels of editing, Tony's instructor had the class review their paragraphs again. This time their purpose was to identify pronoun inconsistencies and weak verbs, particularly passive structures. The instructor first had students go through their own paragraphs and circle all the pronouns in their sentences.

TONY'S PARAGRAPH

Junk food can be bought practically anywhere, including grocery stores, fast-food restaurants, and gas stations. It is usually cheap, maybe because it doesn't have any nutritional value. Some examples are potato chips, cookies, greasy burgers, fries, donuts, candy bars, and sodas. (You) eat (this) stuff and get a sugar or caffeine fix and then get sick. (They) should label (this) stuff better to let people know (we're) wasting (our) money. Instead of (us) buying junk food, nutritional food should be bought.

Next, the students read each other's paragraphs and answered questions provided by the instructor. Rita responded to Tony's draft.

◢ A Classmate Responds

QUESTIONS FOR REVIEW

1. Do the pronouns in each sentence clearly refer to a noun or another pronoun? Which ones do not?
2. Do the pronouns shift from *I* to *you*, *I* to *they*, *we* to *they*, or the like? Which ones?
3. Do the pronouns shift from singular to plural or from plural to singular? Which ones?

Rita's answers helped Tony see why part of his paragraph was not clear.

RITA'S RESPONSES

1. In the second sentence *it* is not clear, and in the fifth sentence *they* is not clear.
2. The fourth sentence has *you*, the fifth has *they*, *we*, and *our*, and the last sentence has *us*. This is confusing to follow.
3. The pronouns change so much, I don't know how to answer this question.

■ A Student Writes

Tony felt confident that with Rita's suggestions he could revise the sentences and make the pronouns consistent. His changes are underlined in the next revision.

TONY'S REVISION

Junk food can be bought practically anywhere, including grocery stores, fast-food restaurants, and gas stations. <u>Junk food</u> is usually cheap, maybe because it doesn't have any nutritional value. Some examples are potato chips, cookies, greasy burgers, fries, donuts, candy bars, and sodas. <u>People</u> eat this stuff and get a sugar or caffeine fix and then get sick. <u>Companies</u> should label this stuff better and let people know <u>they</u> are wasting <u>their</u> money. Instead of <u>people</u> buying junk food, nutritional food should be bought.

For the second step in this level of revision, the students went through their paragraphs and circled all of the forms of *to be* (*is, am, are, was, were, be, been, being*) in their sentences.

TONY'S PARAGRAPH

Junk food can (be) bought practically anywhere, including grocery stores, fast-food restaurants, and gas stations. Junk food (is) usually cheap, maybe because it doesn't have any nutritional value. Some examples (are) potato chips, cookies, greasy burgers, fries, donuts, candy bars, and sodas. People eat this stuff and get a sugar or caffeine fix and then get sick. Companies should label this stuff better and let people know they (are) wasting their money. Instead of people buying junk food, nutritional food should (be) bought.

Next, the students read each other's paragraphs and answered the questions for review. Tony was looking forward to Rita's suggestions.

◢ A Classmate Responds

QUESTIONS FOR REVIEW

1. Do the verbs in each sentence clearly show action? Which ones do not?

2. Do the verbs clearly show who or what performs the action? Which ones do not?
3. Do any of the sentences need different verbs? Which ones?

Rita's answers were brief but helpful.

RITA'S RESPONSES

1. Sentences 1, 2, 3, and 6 don't have verbs that clearly show action.
2. The same sentences don't tell who performs the action.
3. The same sentences need different verbs.

■ A Student Writes

Tony had to spend some time thinking about these suggestions, but he managed to find ways to revise his sentences using active verbs. In addition to changing some verbs, he also decided to change the second sentence. His changes are underlined in the revision that follows.

TONY'S REVISED PARAGRAPH

People can buy junk food practically anywhere, including grocery stores, fast-food restaurants, and gas stations. Junk food does not cost much money and often has no nutritional value. Some examples of nonnutritious foods include potato chips, cookies, hamburgers, french fries, donuts, candy bars, and sodas. People eat this stuff and get a sugar or caffeine fix and then get sick. Companies should label this stuff better and let people know that the purchase of it wastes their money. Instead of buying junk food, people should buy nutritional food.

Tony could see the difference between this draft and the previous draft, and he felt that his paragraph had begun to sound clear and consistent in structure. His instructor had one more level of revision planned for the class. This level is discussed at the end of chapter 9.

Chapter 9

Choosing Words

9a Choosing the Best Verb

When deciding which verb to use in a sentence, choose a strong, active-voice verb that expresses your meaning precisely. Expand your thinking and consider the possible choices and meanings available. Consider your intent as a writer — what feeling do you want to express? Consider your audience — what reaction or response do you want to elicit?

For example, let's examine the following sentence.

Josh *walked* into the room.

The verb *walked* is an acceptable active verb, but let's substitute some verbs that change the meaning and the impact of the sentence to elicit different responses from readers.

Josh *strolled* into the room.

Josh *stumbled* into the room.

Josh *pranced* into the room.

Josh *tiptoed* into the room.

Josh *slinked* into the room.

There are a multitude of verbs that can describe how Josh entered the room. As a writer, you can choose which one to use.

Let's try another example.

The author *is saying* that animals have rights.

157

The verb *is saying* is a progressive form that seems weak in this sentence. Let's substitute some active verbs that give impact to the sentence.

> The author *says* that animals have rights.

> The author *mentions* that animals have rights.

> The author *explains* that animals have rights.

> The author *emphasizes* that animals have rights.

> The author *insists* that animals have rights.

Be creative when choosing verbs. Using the strongest and most precise verb to convey your exact meaning will make your writing lively and keep your readers' interest high.

9b

9b Unnecessary Repetition

Good writers convey their ideas as concisely as possible so that their readers can understand their main ideas. Sometimes, writers repeat words or phrases to maintain coherence, but problems arise when those repetitions interfere with the flow of ideas. Here are some examples.

> The movies today present *many various* examples of sick violence.

> *In addition,* the workers will *also* need uniforms.

In the first example *many* and *various* have the same meaning, so the writer needs to include either *many* or *various,* but not both. In the second example *In addition* and *also* have the same meaning, so, again, the writer needs to choose only one word or phrase.

Writers also must be sure that each sentence states ideas that are not needlessly repeated. Consider these sentences.

> The *snowy* blizzard caused hazardous road conditions and power outages.

Advertisers try to attract consumers *so that the consumers will* buy certain products.

The word *snowy* in the first sentence needlessly repeats the idea stated in the word *blizzard*. The second sentence needs to be rephrased to avoid repeating *consumers*.

Advertisers try to attract *consumers to buy* certain products.

Strive for the simplest, most concise way to express your ideas.

9c Wordy or Inflated Phrases

9c

Wordy or **inflated phrases** can often be eliminated or reworked without changing the meaning of a sentence. Inflated phrases usually state an idea that is implied.

I believe that animals have rights and should be treated with respect.

The phrase *I believe that* is unnecessary because the reader assumes that the writer believes what he or she has written.

Constructions with *it* are often wordy and can be deleted.

It appears that the importance of voting in an election should not be overlooked.

The introductory phrase *It appears that* adds nothing to the meaning of the sentence and, in fact, weakens its impact. The phrase should be eliminated.

Sometimes, writers use two or more words when one word would do.

On account of the rain, we will have to postpone the picnic.

On account can easily be changed to *because,* which is more concise.

Because of the rain, we will have to postpone the picnic.

Being that is always incorrect; use *since* or *because* instead.

Being that the music had a good beat, people danced for hours.

Replace *being that* with *since*.

Since the music had a good beat, people danced for hours.

Here are some inflated phrases and the words you can substitute for them.

INSTEAD OF	USE
on account	because, since
due to the fact that	because, since
being that	because, since
in the neighborhood of	about, near
a lot of instances	often
the idea as to whether	whether
a great number	many
it is necessary to assume the fact that	[avoid completely]

9d Appropriate Language

9d-1 Levels of Formality

The level of formality you choose depends on the audience, the purpose, and often the form of the writing. **Formal language** is an impersonal, standard usage that is sometimes abstract. **Informal language** is personal and sometimes casual. The following examples illustrate the variation within each category.

MOST FORMAL	MOST INFORMAL
legal and government documents	phone messages letters to friends

technical and scientific reports	personal journal entries
medical documents	newspaper articles
scholarly journal articles	popular culture journal articles
political speeches	

Some writing has a combination of both levels of formality; however, there is usually a clear distinction between the two. For example, if you write to a judge to contest a speeding ticket, you should choose a level of formality different from the level you use to explain the ticket to a friend.

FORMAL: TO A JUDGE

I wish to contest the ticket that I received on 24 November 1991. I do not deserve this ticket because my speedometer was not working correctly, and I could not tell how fast I was going.

9d

Notice the use of the verb *contest* and the deliberate omission of the word *speeding*. The language is simple and to the point.

When you write to a friend, though, you will be informal.

INFORMAL: TO A FRIEND

Would you believe I got a speeding ticket last Sunday just because my speedometer decided to take a hike?

Notice the use of the term *speeding* and the use of the cliché *take a hike*. This language is obviously directed to someone who knows you and who would understand how you feel about the issue.

Unless your audience specifically allows or expects informal writing (like family, friends, or peers), you need to use formal language that creates a distance between you and the reader and gives an objective tone to your writing. Academic and professional writing usually needs to be formal. The following suggestions will help you create a formal piece of writing.

1. Eliminate the second-person pronoun *you*. *You* is used only when the writer and the audience have a close relationship or when the writer presents directions or steps to follow. Use the third-person pronoun *they* when referring to people in general.

INFORMAL You need to learn about the rights of animals.

FORMAL People [or *they*] need to learn about the rights of animals.

2. Eliminate the use of the first-person pronoun *I* except when referring to personal experience. Use the collective *we* instead.

INFORMAL To help homeless people, I can use my understanding of how it feels to be lonely, hungry, and afraid.

FORMAL To help homeless people, we can use our understanding of how it feels to be lonely, hungry, and afraid.

OR People can use their understanding of how it feels to be lonely, hungry, and afraid to help homeless people.

3. Do not overuse contractions. In most college writing moderate use of contractions is acceptable.

INFORMAL We can't help those people who don't want help.

FORMAL People cannot help those who do not want help.

9d-2 Jargon

Jargon is a specialized vocabulary used by people within a particular group, trade, discipline, or job. Writers (as well as speakers) should use jargon carefully and sparingly, since it is difficult for general readers to understand.

The following sentence, for instance, is acceptable for a medical audience but not for a general audience.

The *hematoma* you have *sustained* has *precipitated* the use of *cold compresses* to reduce *edema*.

The sentence should be rephrased for a general audience.

The *bruise* you *have needs* an *icepack* to reduce *swelling*.

The use of jargon can imply elitism on the part of the writer as well as complicate sentence structure, thus limiting

9d

communication. For general audiences writers avoid the use of jargon.

9d-3 Wordy Language

Wordy language is characterized by unnecessarily long words and flowery words or phrases. Meanings get lost in the excessive wording.

WORDY

Speakers should eschew obfuscation, especially when amongst those whose willingness to partake of myriad conceptualizations is evident.

This sentence should be reworded to eliminate wordiness.

9d

CLEAR

Speakers should avoid confusing words, especially when they are around people willing to learn new ideas.

9d-4 Euphemisms

A **euphemism** is a word or phrase that takes the place of another word or phrase to soften its impact, confuse its meaning, evade reality, or present a false impression. While euphemisms can be appropriate and are often preferred for creative, political, or humorous purposes, they should be used carefully and sparingly.

The following lists give some examples of euphemisms and their meanings.

EUPHEMISM	MEANING
active euthanasia	intentional killing
chemically dependent	addicted
home plaque removal instrument	toothbrush
maintenance operator	janitor
passed away	died
previously owned automobile	used car
resilient vinyl flooring	linoleum

senior citizen	old person
stretch the truth	lie
surgical strike	bombing
temporarily disoriented	lost
termination	killing
uncontrolled contact with the ground	plane crash
vegetarian leather	vinyl

A careful writer will use the words in the second column when writing for a general audience.

9d-5 Clichés

9d

A cliché is an overused phrase that has very little impact in writing. Writers should avoid using clichés, substituting instead fresh, vivid images that convey information accurately and concretely. The following list gives some common clichés that careful writers should replace with their own words.

all work and no play
avoid it like the plague
bent out of shape
better late than never
burn the midnight oil
in the final analysis
in this day and age
it goes without saying
last but not least
live on a shoestring
only time will tell
to make a long story short

9d-6 Idioms

An **idiom** is a phrase that has a meaning other than the one that individual words define—a meaning often based on the context in which the phrase appears. For example, the idiom *need a lift* has different meanings depending on context. It can mean

"I need a ride," or "I need a boost," or "I need my spirits uplifted."

An idiom can also be a combination of words that must be used together to convey a clear meaning. Dictionaries often include the correct forms of common idioms. Idioms should be used carefully and correctly. The following list gives some commonly misused idioms and their correct forms.

INCORRECT	CORRECT
agree to	agree with
angry at	angry with
apologize about	apologize for
die from	die of
different than	different from
ever now and then	every now and then
excepting for	except for
identical to	identical with
intend on doing	intend to do
off of	off
plan on	plan to
sure and	sure to
try and see	try to see
a whole nother	a whole other, another

9d

9d-7 Slang and Nonstandard English

Slang is a form of the language that is extremely informal and usually understood only by the particular group that uses it. For example, someone who grew up in the 1950s might refer to a good movie as *cool*, someone from the 1960s as *neat*, and someone from the 1980s as *awesome* or *bad*, because those slang terms were acceptable or popular at those particular times. Some slang terms are acceptable in informal conversations or in very informal writings but rarely in academic or professional writing.

Here are some examples of slang terms and the standard words you should use instead.

SLANG	STANDARD
guys	men
kids	children

porno	pornography
tv	television
the paper	the newspaper
booze	alcoholic beverage, beer, wine, and so on

Another form of English, called **nonstandard English,** is often spoken by people within a specific social or cultural group. Acceptable in speech, this form of the language is usually not acceptable in academic or professional writing.

NONSTANDARD

They *ain't* going to arrive on time because they *was* asleep too long.

Joe *done been gone to* Germany so long he *be missed* by *us all.*

9d

These sentences should be revised to standard English.

STANDARD

They *aren't* going to arrive on time because they *were* asleep too long.

Joe *has been in* Germany so long he *is* missed by *all of us.*

OR Joe *has been in* Germany so long *that we all miss him.*

9d-8 Sexist Language

Sexist language promotes narrow thinking and encourages the continuation of gender stereotypes. For instance, the following list gives stereotypical male and female roles.

MALE ROLES	FEMALE ROLES
doctors	nurses
lawyers	secretaries
mechanics	telephone operators
executives	restaurant servers
pilots	teachers

In sexist usage words like *doctor, lawyer, mechanic, executive,* and *pilot* are often followed by the pronouns *he, him,* and *his;* whereas words like *nurse, secretary, telephone operator, restaurant server,* and *teacher* are oftened followed by the pronouns *she, her,* and *hers.*

One way writers can eliminate implied gender stereotypes is to use combined pronouns (*he or she, him or her, his or hers*) or plural forms of the career-related words followed by plural pronouns (*they, them, their, theirs*).

A doctor sees *his* or *her* patients every three weeks.

Some doctors see *their* patients every three weeks.

A teacher gives *his* or *her* students homework every night.

Some teachers give *their* students homework every night.

9d

Whenever possible, revise your sentences so that you do not have to use a pronoun.

Some doctors see patients every three weeks.

That doctor sees patients every three weeks.

Some traditional masculine or feminine terms have recently become inappropriate and have been rephrased to eliminate any reference to gender stereotypes.

TRADITIONAL USAGE	CURRENT USAGE
alderman	alderperson
businessman	executive
chairman	chair, facilitator
fireman	firefighter
forefathers	ancestors
mailman	mail carrier
man	humanity
policeman	police officer
salesman	sales representative, salesclerk, salesperson
waiter/waitress	food server, server
workman	worker

9e   Exact Language

9e-1   Concrete and Abstract Nouns

Concrete nouns specify definite meanings, usually based on a person's sensory perception—words like *table, salty, green, mushy, loud*. **Abstract nouns** express ideas, qualities, and feelings—such as *democracy, hope,* and *anger*. Although concrete nouns are sometimes preferred for clarity, writers often use a combination of concrete and abstract nouns to convey information effectively.

9e

> The *cowboy* [concrete] fell off his *horse* [concrete] with *dignity*. [abstract]

Abstract nouns (like *ethics, love, desire, loneliness, anger*) are acceptable when used with concrete nouns for clarification. The use of abstract nouns makes writing seem formal and, sometimes, objective. But abstract nouns used alone can make writing seem vague.

> VAGUE
>
> In his campaign speeches Senator Gore focused on *environmental issues*.
>
> Brad's *push* for ethics in the workplace has caused many good *things* to happen.

These sentences become clearer when concrete, specific examples are added.

> REVISED FOR CLARITY
>
> In his campaign speeches Senator Gore focused on environmental issues like *air pollution, the destruction of the rain forests,* and *water contamination*. [concrete details added]
>
> Brad's *discussions with people* about ethics in the workplace have caused workers *to stop stealing, to stop falsifying work hours,* and *to stop taking unnecessary sick days*. [concrete details added]

9e-2 Denotation and Connotation

The **denotation** of a word is its lexical or dictionary definition. The **connotation** is the implied, emotion-laden meaning placed on or indicated by the word. For example, the word *communism* has a limited denotation: a classless system with communal ownership. The connotation, however, depends on the context and on the age of the person using the word. For instance, people who grew up in the 1940s and 1950s have a negative emotional meaning for the word *communism*, which was an evil force to be stopped.

Be aware of both the lexical definitions and implied meanings of the words you choose so the reader will understand the exact meaning you intend to convey. Whether or not you emphasize the connotations of words, make sure that the implied meanings are those that you intend and that they match the context, voice, and tone of your writing.

9e

9e-3 Figures of Speech

Figures of speech make comparisons (expressed or implied) between different things. They make the language fun and help to make abstract ideas more concrete. The following list explains the most common types of figures of speech and gives examples of their use.

HYPERBOLE A hyperbole gives a deliberate exaggeration.

That grocery sack weighs *a ton*.
Some fast-food restaurants sell *garbage*.
There were *ten million people* at Jack's party Friday.

IRONY Irony states the opposite of the intended meaning.

When Sam looked outside and saw the rain mixed with sleet, he said "*What a gorgeous day it is!*"

METAPHOR A metaphor implies a comparison between two dissimilar things.

Life is a *game*.
Mother Earth is calling to me.

OXYMORON An oxymoron combines contradictory terms.

honest thief
eloquent silence

SIMILE A simile shows a direct comparison by using *like* or *as*.

soft as a kitten
stubborn as a mule
feels like leather

9f   Using a Dictionary

A **dictionary** is a valuable tool for writers because it includes not only the correct spellings and definitions of words but also pronunciations, plural forms, past-participle and progressive (*-ing*) endings of verbs, syllabications, and word origins. College students need a collegiate dictionary like *The American Heritage Dictionary*.

The following typical dictionary entry illustrates the various parts of a definition.

Also included in most dictionaries is a pronunciation key at the bottom of each page. This pronunciation key gives suggestions on how to use the vowel and consonant symbols shown in the parentheses right after the words listed.

9f-1   To Find the Meaning of a Word

Readers use a dictionary to check the meaning of a word if they are not sure how it is used in a sentence. (See the sample entry in section 9f.) Writers can use a dictionary to make sure that they have used a word correctly. Usually, the first definition listed is the one most commonly used.

[SAMPLE DICTIONARY ENTRY]

pronunciation key   parts of verb   type of verb

definitions

a•gree (ə-grē′) *v.* **agreed, agreeing, agrees.** *—intr.* **1.** To grant consent: accede. Used with the infinitive: *He agreed to accompany us.* **2.** To come into or be in accord: *The copy agrees with the original.* **3.** To be of one opinion. Often used with *with: "Didst thou not agree with me for a penny?"* (Matthew 20:13). **4.** To come to an understanding or to terms. Used with *about* or *on: Is it possible to agree on such great problems?* **5.** To be suitable: appropriate. Used with *with: Spicy food does not agree with him.* **6.** *Grammar.* To correspond in gender, number, case, or person. *—tr.* To grant or concede. Used with a noun clause: *He agreed that we should go* —See Synonyms at **assent.** [Middle English *agreen,* from Old French *agreer,* from Vulgar Latin *aggrātāre* (unattested), to be pleasing to :*ad-,* to + *grātus,* pleasing, beloved, agreeable (see **gwere-**¹ in Appendix*).]

etymology (*word origin*)

Synonyms: *agree, conform, harmonize, accord, correspond, coincide.* These verbs all indicate compatible relationship between people or things. *Agree* may indicate mere lack of incongruity or discord, but often it suggests acceptance of ideas or actions and thus accommodation. *Conform* stresses close resemblance in form, thought, or basic characteristics, sometimes the result of accommodation to established standards. *Harmonize* implies a relationship of unlike things combined or arranged to make a pleasing whole. *Accord* implies close similarity between things or harmonious relationship or both. *Correspond* refers either to actual similarity in form or nature or to similarity in function of unlike things. *Coincide* stresses exact agreement in space, time, or thought.

synonyms

9f

— From *The American Heritage Dictionary,* p. 26.

[EXAMPLE OF PRONUNCIATION KEY]

\ə\ abut \ᵊ\ kitten, F table \ər\ further \a\ ash \ā\ ace \ä\ cot, cart \au̇\ out \ch\ chin \e\ bet \ē\ easy \g\ go \i\ hit \ī\ ice \j\ job \ŋ\ sing \ō\ go \ȯ\ law \ȯi\ boy \th\ thin \t͟h\ the \ü\ loot \u̇\ foot \y\ yet \zh\ vision \à, k̲, ⁿ, œ, œ̄, ᴜe, ᴜ̄e, ᵞ\ *see* Guide to Pronunciation

— *Webster's Ninth New Collegiate Dictionary*

9f-1a Slang

Some words that you use in everyday speech are listed in the dictionary as slang and are generally not acceptable in formal, academic writing.

NOT ACCEPTABLE	ACCEPTABLE
goofy	different, unusual, silly
guy	man, person, individual
kid	child

9f-1b Vulgar or Offensive Meanings

Many dictionaries also label definitions as **vulgar** when the words used in that sense are not acceptable in polite communication. For example, the word *snot* is listed as having the following vulgar or offensive meanings: "devious, spiteful, and mean."

9f-1c Obsolete and Archaic Meanings

You will sometimes find **obsolete words** (words that are no longer used) listed in dictionaries. For example, the obsolete word *pigsney*, which means "a darling," is not used in modern American English.

You will also find some words or definitions listed as **archaic** — the term is still in use but is outdated and not preferred. For example, the archaic word *ere* means "previous to" or "before." Although *ere* is still used in poetry, the word *before* is used in everyday writing.

9f-2 To Check the Origin of a Word

Most dictionaries indicate word origins in brackets [ ] at the end of the definition (see the sample entry in section 9f). You will find the information fascinating as well as useful for gaining insight into how modern meanings have originated. For example, the word *tentacle* originates from the Latin word *tentare*, which means "to touch."

9f-3 To Find the Synonym of a Word

Some dictionaries list **synonyms** (words that have the same meaning as the listed word) at the end of the definition entry (see the sample entry in section 9f). They also may include sentence examples for each synonym, which can help you find the word with the connotation you are looking for to express your meaning precisely.

9f-4 To Check the Spelling of a Word

You can use a dictionary to check the spelling of words (see the sample entry in section 9f). If you do not know how to spell a particular word, try "sounding out" different letter combinations. Look up the different letter combinations in the dictionary to help you to find the correct spelling.

EXAMPLE 1

Check the spelling of *separate* by sounding out the syllables.

sep	sounds like a short *e*
a	sounds like a short *u* or a short *a*
rate	sounds like a long *a*

Look up the different combinations.

9f

EXAMPLE 2

Check the spelling of *specific* by sounding out the syllables.

spe	sounds like a long *e* or a short *u*
ci	sounds like an *s* or *c* and a short *i*
fic	sounds like an *f* or *ph* and a short *i*

Look up the different combinations.

With several attempts and with the help of the pronunciation key at the bottom of each dictionary page, you should be able to find the correct spellings of many words.

9f-4a American vs. British Spellings

Most dictionaries list both American and British spellings of many common words. Here are some examples.

AMERICAN	BRITISH
center	centre
color	colour
favor	favour
neighbor	neighbour
realize	realise
theater	theatre

Most instructors prefer that you use the American spellings of these words.

9f-4b Preferred Spellings

Many dictionaries list two or more spellings for particular words. When the spellings are listed together before a definition, the first one listed is usually the preferred spelling. The second spelling is referred to as the *variant spelling*.

PREFERRED	VARIANT
ax	axe
backward	backwards
judgment	judgement
theater	theatre
toward	towards

9g

9g   Spelling

When you use the dictionary to check the spelling of a word, here are a few common spelling rules to keep in mind.

1. *Spell words with* i *before* e *except after* c.

believe	conceive
relief	receive
thief	

Exception: If *ie* has a long *a* sound (as in *may*), spell the word with *ei*.

eight	reindeer
feint	vein
neighbor	weigh
reign	

Finally, other common exceptions are as listed next.

feisty	seize
height	seizure
heir	their

heist   weird
leisure

2. *For words ending in a consonant plus e, drop the e when adding* -ing.

cope   coping
enforce   enforcing
hope   hoping
live   living
rave   raving
stumble   stumbling

3. *For words ending in a vowel plus y, keep the y when adding* -s, -ed, *or* -ing.

employ   play   toy
employs   plays   toys
employed   played   toyed

Some exceptions follow.

pay   say
pays   says
paid   said

9g

4. *For words ending in a consonant plus y, change the y to i and add* -es *or* -ed.

study   terrify   try
studies   terrifies   tries
studied   terrified   tried

Keep the y when you add -ing.

studying   terrifying   trying

5. *For words with one syllable ending in a vowel plus a consonant, double the last letter when adding* -ed *or* -ing.

grin   plot
grinned   plotted
grinning   plotting

6. *For foreign language words, use the singular and plural forms given in the list.*

SINGULAR	PLURAL
analysis	analyses
crisis	crises
criterion	criteria

curriculum	curricula
datum	data
medium	media
syllabus	syllabi

7. *For plural forms of hyphenated nouns, add an* -s *to the main noun even if it is not at the end of the hyphenated word.*

father-in-law [singular]
fathers-in-law [plural]

8. *For singular nouns, add* -s *or* -es.

SINGULAR	PLURAL
book	books
brain	brains
lunch	lunches

For nouns that end in ay, ey, *or* oy, *add* -s.

SINGULAR	PLURAL
bay	bays
key	keys
monkey	monkeys
toy	toys

For nouns that end in y *with a consonant before it, change the* y *to* i *and add* -es.

SINGULAR	PLURAL
company	companies
energy	energies
fly	flies
tendency	tendencies

9g

■ A Student Writes

After class discussions on word choice Tony's instructor had the class review their paragraphs about junk food for appropriate language, use of abstract and concrete nouns, and correct spelling.

TONY'S PARAGRAPH

People can buy junk food practically anywhere, including grocery stores, fast-food restaurants, and gas stations. Junk food does not cost much money and often has no nutritional value. Some examples of nonnutritious foods include potato chips, cookies, hamburgers, french fries, donuts, candy bars, and sodas. People eat this stuff and get a sugar or caffeine fix and then get sick. Companies should label this stuff better and let people know that the purchase of it wastes their money. Instead of buying junk food, people should buy nutritional food.

The instructor provided a handout with suggestions for review. Once again, Tony asked Rita for some suggestions.

◪ A Classmate Responds

QUESTIONS FOR REVIEW

1. Does the language sound appropriate for the audience? Which words do not?
2. Are there enough concrete nouns? Are there enough (or too many) abstract nouns? Which ones are not clear?
3. Do any words seem to be misspelled? Which ones?

Rita's answers were helpful to Tony and reassured him that his paragraph was almost ready to submit to his instructor.

RITA'S RESPONSES

1. The word *stuff* doesn't fit. Everything else sounds okay.
2. The only unclear part is in the last sentence. What do you mean by *nutritional food?*
3. I don't know if *caffeine* is spelled correctly.

■ A Student Writes

Tony thanked Rita for her suggestions and began to revise his paragraph, keeping her answers in mind. He made the

changes she suggested and looked up the word *caffeine* in his
dictionary. He had, in fact, spelled it correctly. His revised paragraph follows, with changes underlined.

TONY'S REVISED PARAGRAPH

People can buy junk food practically anywhere, including
grocery stores, fast-food restaurants, and gas stations. Junk food
does not cost much money and often has no nutritional value.
Some examples of nonnutritious foods include potato chips,
cookies, hamburgers, french fries, donuts, candy bars, and sodas. People eat this <u>kind of food</u> and get a sugar or caffeine fix
and then get sick. Companies should label <u>their products</u> and let
people know that the purchase of <u>these products</u> wastes their
money. Instead of buying junk food, people should buy nutritional foods <u>such as meats, vegetables, and dairy products</u>.

Tony still had to proofread his paragraph to look for punctuation and mechanical errors. This last part of the writing and
revising process will be discussed at the ends of the chapters in
Part Four.

Chapter 10

Commonly
Confused Words

a, an

Use *a* before a word that begins with a consonant or a consonant sound.

 a stereo *a* horse *a* book

Use *an* before a word that begins with a vowel or a silent *h*.

 an orange *an* honor

For further discussion on articles, see section 8d-4.

accept, except

Accept means "to receive something" or "to approve of something."

 She *accepts* your invitation

Except as a preposition means "not to include"; as a verb, it means "to exclude."

 Everyone *except* Sam was invited.

adapt, adopt

Adapt means "to adjust to something" or "to change."

 You may find it difficult to *adapt* to this unusual weather.

Adopt means "to gain legal custody" or "to use something as your own."

 Jim and Susan have *adopted* a baby girl.

 Some states have *adopted* new tax laws this year.

advice, advise

Advice is a noun that means "words of counsel."

John needs *advice* on buying a car.

Advise is a verb that means "to give counsel."

Please *advise* him of his rights.

affect, effect

Affect is most often used as a verb meaning "to change" or "to influence."

How did the pay raise *affect* your life-style?

Affect can also be used as a noun (in health sciences or in psychology) to mean a person's facial expression or an emotion.

John's *affect* makes it difficult for us to tell if he is happy or sad.

Effect is most often used as a noun meaning "a result or a change that has taken place."

Too much rain has had a terrible *effect* on crops.

Effect can also be used as a verb meaning "to cause."

That new tax law *effected* a change in our tax payment.

a little, alittle

A little is the only correct form.

all right, alright

All right is the only correct form.

Sally decided it would be *all right* to accept the new job.

all together, altogether

All together means "a group action" or "something done collectively."

The committee members were *all together* at the last meeting.

Altogether means "entirely."

He was not *altogether* certain of a career choice.

a lot, alot

A lot is the only correct form.

already, all ready

Already means "before" or "by this time."

John had *already* eaten.

All ready means "completely prepared" to do something.

The restaurant was *all ready* for its grand opening.

among, between

Use *among* when referring to three or more people or things.

Hank spent his afternoons *among* friends at the student center.

Use *between* when referring to two people or things.

This secret is *between* you and me.

anxious, eager

Anxious means "nervous" or "full of dread."

She was *anxious* about the final exam in her history class.

Eager means "happily awaiting."

Sam was *eager* to meet his new mother-in-law.

awful, awfully

Use *awful* as an adjective.

That horror movie was *awful* and much too violent.

Use *awfully* as an adverb that describes how much.

Larry was *awfully* shaken after the canoe accident.

awhile, a while

Use *awhile* as an adverb to indicate how long.

The twins decided to stay home *awhile*.

10

Comm.
Conf.
Words

Use *a while* as the object of a preposition.

Let's go swimming for *a while*.

bad, badly

Use *bad* as an adjective.

He was *bad* in school today.

Use *badly* as an adverb that means very much or in a bad manner.

Ruth *badly* wanted to go to Europe.

The house down the street was *badly* constructed.

being as, being that

Use *since* or *because* instead of these incorrect phrases.

INCORRECT *Being that* it is so late, the store will probably be closed.

CORRECT *Since* it is so late, the store will probably be closed.

beside, besides

Beside means "next to."

The husky sleeps *beside* the air conditioner where she can stay cool.

Besides means "other than."

Two people *besides* Jim are going skating tomorrow.

between, among

See among, between.

cannot

Always write *cannot* as one word, not two.

can't hardly, not hardly, hardly

Hardly is the only correct form. *Can't hardly* and *not hardly* are double negatives and are incorrect.

Jack can *hardly* control his excitement about his vacation.

capital, capitol

Capital (with an *a*) means a city that is a seat of government or a large amount of money or wealth.

Washington, D.C., is the *capital* of the United States.

Capitol (with an *o*) means a building used by a legislative body.

The view from the *Capitol* in Washington, D.C., is spectacular.

cite, sight, site

Cite means "to indicate the source of information" or "to document."

Always *cite* some reputable source to support an argument.

Sight means "vision."

At 60 Joanie's *sight* is better than most people's at 30.

Site means "a location."

The new mall will be built on a *site* close to the freeway.

complement, compliment

Complement as a verb means "to complete."

The alto and tenor sections of the choir *complement* each other nicely.

Complement as a noun means "compatible."

Navy blue is a nice *complement* to pale blue.

Compliment as a verb means "to praise."

Sally *complimented* the luncheon speakers on their fine presentations.

Compliment as a noun means "a flattering statement."

Susan appreciated the *compliment* she received yesterday.

conscience, conscious

Conscience means "a person's sense of right or wrong."

Joe's *conscience* bothered him after he stole that car.

10
Comm.
Conf.
Words

Conscious is an adjective meaning "awake" or "aware of something."

Was she really *conscious* during that tooth extraction?

could of

Could of is an incorrect form of *could have*.

Today's picnic *could have* been perfect if the weather had stayed clear.

etc., ect.

Etc. is the only correct abbreviation for *et cetera,* which means "and so forth."

farther, further

Use *farther* to refer to a measurable distance.

Mr. Smith traveled *farther* last year than his wife did.

Use *further* to refer to immeasurable amounts.

If you need *further* assistance with your class schedule, please talk to an academic advisor.

good, well

Use *good* only as an adjective.

That blackberry pie was *good*.

Use *well* as an adjective or as an adverb.

After his long illness, Sam is finally *well*. [adjective]

He did his job *well*. [adverb that tells how]

hardly, can't hardly, not hardly

See **can't hardly**.

himself, hisself

Himself is the correct form.

in, into

Use *in* to mean "in place."

The book is *in* the library.

Use *into* to indicate movement from one place to another.

She went *into* the movie theater.

is when, is where

Both terms are incorrectly used as part of a definition.

INCORRECT A stalemate *is when* there is a standoff.

CORRECT A stalemate *is* a standoff between two opponents.

its, it's

Its is a possessive pronoun.

The cat licked *its* paw.

It's is a contraction for *it is*.

It's raining.

lead, led

Use *lead* as a verb to mean "to give direction to" or "to have authority over" someone or something.

He will *lead* the clowns in the parade.

Lead (short *e* sound) as a noun refers to the element lead.

lead poisoning

Use *led* as the past-tense form of *to lead*.

Joan *led* the chorus in a wonderful rendition of "Send in the Clowns."

lend, loan

Use *lend* as a verb.

The bank *lends* money to a select group of people.

10

Comm.
Conf.
Words

Use *loan* as a noun.

> I wonder how much money John plans to get for his car *loan*.

lie, lay

Use *lie* to mean "to recline" (principal parts: *lie, lay, lain*).

> She decided to *lie* down and relax.

Use *lay* to mean "to place an object" (principal parts: *lay, laid, laid*).

> Mr. Jones *laid* the stone foundation for his house yesterday.

loose, lose

Loose is an adjective meaning "not attached securely."

> That bolt is *loose* enough to cause the shelf to fall.

Lose is a verb meaning "to misplace" or "to be unsuccessful."

> How many people *lose* their car keys at least once?

may of

May of is an incorrect form of *may have*.

> Jackie *may have* already gone home from work.

might of

Might of is an incorrect form of *might have*.

> The whale population *might have* disappeared if people hadn't started to be concerned about mammals' lives again.

pacific, specific

Pacific always refers to an ocean or area: Pacific Ocean, Pacific Northwest.
Specific refers to something particular.

> The students decided that they needed *specific* instructions to complete the homework assignment.

passed, past

Passed is a verb (past tense of *to pass*).

Most students are glad when they have *passed* English Composition.

Past is a noun that means "something that has already happened," an adverb that means "to go beyond," or an adjective that means "not current."

In the *past* students had to write six essays for this class. [noun]

Jeremy drove *past* his high school. [adverb]

The *past* few years have been a time of adventure. [adjective]

prejudice, prejudiced

Use *prejudice* as a noun or a verb.

Prejudice is a bias against a group of people. [noun]

Those people *prejudice* their views of others because of race and religion. [verb]

Use *prejudiced* as an adjective.

Prejudiced people find it difficult to see others as individuals.

principal, principle

Use *principal* as a noun to refer to the head of a school or to money.

A *principal's* job in any school is a difficult one.

Once you pay off the *principal* and the interest on your mortgage, you will have to pay only the taxes each month.

Use *principal* as an adjective to refer to something of major importance.

Getting back to the basics is the *principal* change we need in our school system.

Use *principle* as a noun to refer to a moral, a code of ethics, or a law.

Telling lies, even minor ones, goes against Susan's *principles*.

real, really

Real is an adjective that means "authentic, actual, or genuine."

The *real* color of a ripe orange is not the bright orange we see in grocery stores.

Real is sometimes used as a synonym for *very;* this usage is not acceptable in academic writing. Instead, use the adverb *really*.

Stephen was *really* excited about his new job at the zoo.

reason, because

Never use these two words together as in "the reason is because."

The *reason* she went home is that she was tired.

She went home *because* she was tired.

10
Comm.
Conf.
Words

reason why

Use *reason* by itself; *reason why* is redundant.

The *reason* I never told you was that I thought you would be angry.

should of

Should of is an incorrect form of *should have*.

The swallows *should have* flown south by now to avoid the cold winter.

sit, set

Use *sit* to mean "to take a seat" (principal parts: *sit, sat, sat*).

Tomorrow we will *sit* down and have a long chat.

Use *set* to mean "to place an object" (principal parts: *set, set, set*).

Tonight is Jane's turn to *set* the table for dinner.

suppose to, supposed to

Supposed to is the correct form.

Students are *supposed to* do their homework on time.

than, then

Use *than* to indicate a comparison.

The Doberman is larger *than* the cocker spaniel.

Use *then* to indicate time.

Finish your test, and *then* relax.

their, there, they're

Their is a plural possessive pronoun.

Their books are quite expensive.

There indicates a place.

Sit over *there* by the fireplace.

There can also be used as an expletive.

There are several bookstores that sell French magazines.

They're is a contraction for *they are*.

They're going to Toronto for their vacation this year.

10
Comm.
Conf.
Words

theirselves, themselves, themself

Themselves is the only correct form.

The girls felt the need to convince *themselves* that they were right.

til, till, until

Until is the only correct form to use for a time reference. *Til* is a sesame plant. *Till* can be a verb meaning "to plow" or a noun meaning "a drawer in which to keep money."

to, too, two

To is a preposition.

Jim went *to* the store and bought some meat for lunch.

To is also part of a verb infinitive.

The music was loud enough *to break* windows.

Too is an adverb meaning "excessively" or "very."

Susan was simply *too* tired to think clearly during the final exam.

In addition, *too* can mean "also."

> Other students in Susan's class decided they were pretty tired, *too*.

Two is a number.

> That book has *two* fascinating chapters on the origins of the English language.

use to, used to

Used to is the correct form.

> You'll find it easy to get *used to* this beautiful weather we have had recently.

wait for, wait on

Wait for means "to anticipate" or "to stay in place."

> I *waited for* Tom at the store for at least 40 minutes.

Wait on means "to provide service."

> The server has learned how to *wait on* customers who are often rude.

who, whom

Use *who* as a subject.

> *Who* can sing the loudest in that choir?

> He is the one *who* decided which puppy to buy.

Use *whom* as the object of a preposition or as the object of a verb.

> Jim was the person with *whom* I spoke.

> You called *whom* for directions to the party?

who's, whose

Who's is the contraction for *who is*.

> I wonder *who's* captain of the team.

Whose is a possessive pronoun.

> Try to remember *whose* glasses are on the table.

10
Comm.
Conf.
Words

would of

Would of is an incorrect form of *would have*.

Timmy *would have* gone to Europe if he were wealthy.

you all

You all is not acceptable in academic writing.

your, you're

Your is the possessive pronoun.

Your books are in the car.

You're is the contraction for *you are*.

You're only as old as you feel.

■ A Student Writes

After having students write paragraphs on buying a car, Jim Su's instructor spent some class time discussing words that writers commonly confuse. The instructor then had the students read each other's paragraphs to see whether any words were used incorrectly.

JIM'S PARAGRAPH

Buying a car can be an wonderful experience, or it can be a disaster. If people know exactly what kind of car they want, than they will have a easier time dealing with the salesperson. The reason for this is because buyers who can make a decision quickly and easily are less likely to be taken advantage of by a quick-talking salesperson. Alot of people do not realize this, and sometimes they go to buy a car when they have not decided for theirselves what they want. Maybe they are use to buying other things and not worrying about making a firm decision. Maybe their just more comfortable having someone else make their decisions for them. If that's the case, than their car-buying experience may end up being a disaster.

◪ A Classmate Responds

Jim asked his classmate Paul to read his paragraph and answer the questions provided by the instructor.

QUESTIONS FOR REVIEW

1. Do any words look incorrect? Which ones?
2. Do any of the words from the list in chapter 10 appear in the paragraph? Which ones seem to be used incorrectly?

Paul's answers were brief, but they indicated that Jim needed to make a few changes.

PAUL'S RESPONSES

1. Yes — in sentence 4, <u>alot</u> doesn't look right, and <u>theirselves</u> sounds funny.
2. Yes — sentence 1, <u>an</u>
        sentence 2, <u>than, a</u>
        sentence 3, <u>the reason for this is because</u>
        sentence 4, <u>alot, theirselves</u>
        sentence 5, <u>use to</u>
        sentence 6, <u>their</u> (the first one; I think the second one is okay)
        sentence 7, <u>than</u>

■ A Student Writes

Jim found Paul's list helpful and easy to use as he examined his paragraph sentence by sentence. Jim consulted chapter 10 to help him decide which words he needed to change in order to make sure his readers would understand his ideas.

JIM'S REVISED PARAGRAPH

Buying a car can be a wonderful experience, or it can be a disaster. If people know exactly what kind of car they want, then they will have an easier time dealing with the salesperson. The reason for this is that buyers who can make a decision quickly and easily are less likely to be taken advantage of by a quick-talking salesperson. A lot of people do not realize this, and sometimes they go to buy a car when they have not decided for themselves what they want. Maybe they are used to buying other things and not worrying about making a firm decision. Maybe they're just more comfortable having someone else make their decisions for them. If that's the case, then their car-buying experience may end up being a disaster.

Part 4

Punctuation and Mechanics

Part 4   Punctuation and Mechanics

Chapter 11

Commas [,]

A **comma** is a mark of punctuation used within a sentence to separate or to connect the parts of the sentence. This chapter explains some basic rules to follow when you use commas.

11a Independent Clauses

Use a comma to connect two independent clauses with *and, or, nor, for* (used to mean *because*), *but, yet,* and *so*. Be sure to put the comma *before* the connecting word.

> John finally gave Mary a ring, *and* she accepted it graciously.

> Students may want to be different, *but* they do not want to appear strange.

11b Dependent Clauses

Use a comma to connect a dependent clause to the independent clause that follows it.

> *When the train suddenly roared through the tunnel,* it frightened the deer standing on the tracks.

If the independent clause comes *before* the dependent clause, you usually do not need to use a comma between the clauses.

> We enjoy soaking in a hot tub *when we have finished skiing for the day.*

11c   Introductory Words, Phrases, and Clauses

Use a comma after an introductory dependent clause.

As the sun began to turn bright orange in the evening, the ducks waddled next door to take a late swim in the neighbor's pool.

For a list of subordinating conjunctions that introduce dependent clauses, see section 8f-3.

If the dependent clause is short, you may omit the comma.

When it rains she feels tired.

Use a comma to set off long introductory prepositional phrases (preposition plus its object plus any modifiers of the object).

At the public beach yesterday, most of the people were sunbathing.

However, if the prepositional phrase is short, you may omit the comma.

At noon the tide rolled in.

Use a comma after introductory verbs that end in *-ing* and *-ed*, verb infinitives (such as *to swim*), and adjectives that end in *-ed*, as well as introductory phrases that begin with these elements.

Swimming, I noticed that the waves were getting much more forceful.

Hoping to get some exercise, I plunged into the icy water.

Frozen in moments, I ran for my towel.

To get my body warm again, I toweled dry and then ran up and down the beach for almost an hour.

Excited, the winning soccer team decided to celebrate.

Commas are usually needed after transitional words like *however, therefore, thus, moreover, consequently,* and *nevertheless.*

However, the hockey team managed to win the game during overtime.

11d Items in a Series

Use commas to separate items in a series.

The campers warmed themselves with blankets, towels, sleeping bags, and whatever else they could find.

Campers generally enjoy spending time in the outdoors, love sleeping in a tent, and delight in telling stories by a campfire.

Notice that a comma is used before *and* in the last item of the series.

11e Coordinate Adjectives

Use a comma to separate two or more **coordinate adjectives**—adjectives that separately modify the same noun.

Some guard dogs are actually gentle, loving, playful animals.

Coordinate adjectives can be logically connected with *and* (gentle and loving and playful) or can be rearranged without altering the meaning of the statement (loving, gentle, playful animals).

11f Nonrestrictive and Restrictive Elements

A **nonrestrictive word, phrase,** or **clause** does not limit meaning and can be eliminated from the sentence without changing the meaning of the sentence. Use two commas to separate nonrestrictive elements from the rest of the sentence.

> NONRESTRICTIVE The kitten's mother, *the gray tabby,* loved to chase the small dogs in the neighborhood.

The phrase *the gray tabby* does not restrict or limit the meaning of *mother.* To understand the concept of *the kitten's mother,* the reader does not need the information *the gray tabby.* Thus, the phrase can be eliminated without changing the meaning of the sentence.

A **restrictive word, phrase,** or **clause** limits the meaning of the word it modifies. When a restrictive word or clause is removed from the sentence, the meaning of the sentence changes.

> RESTRICTIVE Every student *who received a grade below a C* must take the exam again.

The clause *who received a grade below a C* tells which students must retake the exam. Without this restrictive clause the sentence would mean that all the students had to take the test again.

11g Absolute Phrases

An **absolute phrase** modifies an entire sentence rather than a word or another clause. An absolute phrase includes a noun or pronoun and a participial phrase. Use a comma to separate an absolute phrase from the rest of the sentence.

> *The game having ended in a tie*, the team members walked slowly to the bus. [The participial phrase is *having ended in a tie*.]

11h Transitional Words or Phrases

Use a comma to separate a transitional word or phrase from the rest of the sentence.

Contrary to what the team's supporters thought, the referee declared the last goal unacceptable.

The hockey players, *however*, were furious about this decision.

11i   Direct Quotations

Use a comma to separate a direct quotation from the rest of the sentence.

Mr. Jones, who owns several saddle horses, says, "Animals should be treated with respect."

"Some people don't care about these animals," he said, "but we do."

11j   Dates, Addresses, Titles

Use a comma to separate numbers in a date.

The next book club meeting is September 20, 1991.

Use a comma to separate items in an address.

John moved to 165 Moore Road, Salina, Kansas, last November.

Use a comma to separate a person's name from his or her title.

The letter was addressed to John Smith, Director of Car Sales.

11k

11k   Numbers

Use a comma to separate groups of three digits in a large number.

2,347,930

Do not use commas to separate groups of digits after the decimal point in decimal numbers.

72.0436   10,346.1798

11l   Letter Greetings and Closings

Use a comma after the greeting in a personal letter.

Dear Aunt Lisa,

Also use a comma after the closing in a letter.

Sincerely,
Yours truly,
Your friend,

11m   Comma Errors

11m-1   Comma Splices

Do not use a comma to connect two independent clauses without a coordinating conjunction. This error is called a **comma splice**.

INCORRECT   Some dogs are good pets, others are good protectors. [comma splice]

This fault can be corrected in one of three ways.

CORRECT   Some dogs are good pets. Others are good protectors. [comma changed to a period and two clauses changed to two sentences]

OR   Some dogs are good pets; others are good protectors. [comma changed to a semicolon]

OR Some dogs are good pets, and others are good protectors. [coordinating conjunction added after the comma]

11m-2 Comma between Compound Elements

Do not use a comma to separate compound elements — two subjects, for instance, or two predicates (verb and its complements) — in a sentence.

> INCORRECT The singer gave an outstanding performance, and thanked the members of the orchestra for their skill. [compound predicate]

The phrase following *and* is not an independent clause. It is part of the compound predicate telling us about the subject (the singer). The comma between the two predicates should be omitted.

> CORRECT The singer gave an outstanding performance and thanked the members of the orchestra for their skill.

11m-3 Comma after a Coordinating Conjunction

11m

Do not use a comma after a coordinating conjunction (*and, but, or, nor, so, for, yet*).

> INCORRECT The children had time to sing, and, they had time to play.

Use a comma only before *and* to separate the two independent clauses.

> CORRECT The children had time to sing, and they had time to play.

■ A Student Writes

Tonya Goldstein's instructor had her class review their paragraphs on sports for correct comma usage.

TONYA'S PARAGRAPH

Most sports fans spend their time in the winter and early spring watching basketball games — either college or professional ones. They watch five men (or women) racing from one side of the court to the other, dribbling as fast as possible and shooting from the two-point or three-point line. However I would rather watch ice hockey. Whenever I have the time and the money I like to go to the games to support my home team which is the Toronto Maple Leafs. Watching the face-offs, the incredible skating and the goal shots is really exciting. The most excitement I ever had was to meet one of the players after a game. Although I don't remember his name I do remember what he said to me. "Skating in a hockey game" he said "is like gliding on a star." At the time I thought that was the most poetic statement I had ever heard. I guess I still do.

Tonya felt that her paragraph read well, but she was not sure that commas were used correctly. She asked her classmate Raphael to read it and answer the questions on the handout provided by the instructor.

◪ A Classmate Responds

QUESTIONS FOR REVIEW

1. Do any sentences that include a series of items need commas after any of the items in the series or before the final *and?* Which ones?
2. Do any dependent clauses that begin sentences need commas? Which ones?
3. Do any introductory words need commas? Which ones?
4. If quotations are used, do they need commas? Where?

Raphael's answers gave Tonya some suggestions for correcting comma usage and for improving the paragraph.

RAPHAEL'S RESPONSES

1. Sentences 2 and 5 don't have commas before the word *and.*
2. I think sentence 4 and sentence 7 need commas. Maybe you need one in sentence 9 after "At the time."

3. In sentence 3 you need a comma after "However."
4. There is a quotation in sentence 8, but I don't really know if you need one or two commas.

■ A Student Writes

Tonya read Raphael's answers to the questions and felt relieved that she was not the only person who struggled with comma usage. She followed his suggestions, checked chapter 11 for rules and examples of comma usage, and revised her paragraph.

TONYA'S REVISED PARAGRAPH

Most sports fans spend their time in the winter and early spring watching basketball games — either college or professional ones. They watch five men (or women) racing from one side of the court to the other, dribbling as fast as possible, and shooting from the two-point or three-point line. However, I would rather watch ice hockey. Whenever I have the time and the money, I like to go to the games to support my home team, which is the Toronto Maple Leafs. Watching the face-offs, the incredible skating, and the goal shots is really exciting. The most excitement I ever had was to meet one of the players after a game. Although I don't remember his name, I do remember what he said to me. "Skating in a hockey game," he said, "is like gliding on a star." At the time I thought that was the most poetic statement I had ever heard. I guess I still do.

Chapter 12

Semicolons [;]

12a With Independent Clauses

Use a semicolon to connect two independent clauses that have related ideas.

John finally gave Mary a ring; she accepted it.

Students may want to be different; they do not want to appear strange.

Semicolons work a lot like periods; they form a boundary between two independent clauses.

12b

12b In a Series with Internal Punctuation

Use a semicolon to separate items in a series when there are commas within the items in the series.

Ethics can be viewed as moral, religious ideas; as a person's value system; and as knowledge of the distinction between right and wrong.

Since the first item in the series (*moral, religious ideas*) includes a comma, the only clear way to separate the other items from it is with semicolons.

12c Common Errors

Do not use a semicolon to separate a dependent clause from an independent clause.

> INCORRECT After a long evening away from home; Susan's parents decided to give the baby-sitter a bonus.

A semicolon is illogical here because *After a long evening away from home* is an introductory phrase, not a dependent clause.

> CORRECT After a long evening away from home, Susan's parents decided to give the baby-sitter a bonus.

For more information on introductory elements, see section 11c.

Do not use a semicolon to separate independent clauses connected with a coordinating conjunction (*and, or, nor, but, for, so, yet*).

> INCORRECT Most people think that contact sports do not include games like basketball; but basketball can get pretty rough.

The correct punctuation here is a comma.

> CORRECT Most people think that contact sports do not include games like basketball, but basketball can get pretty rough.

The exception to this rule (see section 12b) is that a semicolon is used to separate items in a series when there are commas within the items in the series.

> There are specialty magazines for various types of sports such as tennis, golf, and car racing; for specific kinds of games such as crossword puzzles, video games, and computer games; and for different types of cooking such as Chinese, Italian, and French.

■ A Student Writes

Lee Perugino's instructor had his class review their paragraphs about a winter activity for correct semicolon usage.

LEE'S PARAGRAPH

Camping is one of those winter activities that requires the proper equipment if you want to enjoy yourself. You need a tent that can withstand wind and snow, a sleeping bag, preferably one that can withstand low temperatures, a stove, and a lantern, battery or propane. With the right equipment you at least have a chance of being comfortable in the cold, however, you need more than just "props" to handle camping in the winter. You also need an understanding of your own physical tolerance as well as an understanding of the real dangers; such as frostbite and hypothermia.

Lee wasn't sure how to use semicolons, so he asked Alice to check his draft for problems. Alice used the questions the instructor provided to check Lee's paragraph.

◢ A Classmate Responds

QUESTIONS FOR REVIEW

1. Are you confused by any sentences that include commas? Which ones?
2. Do any sentences use commas instead of semicolons to connect two independent clauses? Which ones?
3. Are any semicolons used to connect a dependent clause to an independent clause? Which ones?

Alice's answers to the questions told Lee that he needed to make a few changes in his punctuation.

ALICE'S RESPONSES

1. Sentence 2 is confusing.
2. Sentence 3.

3. I think the semicolon in sentence 4 is wrong. That last part is not an independent clause.

■ A Student Writes

Lee used Alice's suggestions to revise his paragraph.

LEE'S REVISED PARAGRAPH

Camping is one of those winter activities that requires the proper equipment if you want to enjoy yourself. You need a tent that can withstand wind and snow; a sleeping bag, preferably one that can withstand low temperatures; a stove; and a lantern, battery or propane. With the right equipment you at least have a chance of being comfortable in the cold; however, you need more than just "props" to handle camping in the winter. You also need an understanding of your own physical tolerance as well as an understanding of the real dangers, such as frostbite and hypothermia.

Chapter 13

Colons [:]

13a To Introduce an Example or an Explanation

Use a colon after an independent clause that introduces an example or an explanation.

The magician knew the secrets to holding the audience's attention: illusion and sleight of hand.

13b To Introduce a List

Use a colon to introduce a list.

Writers need specific equipment: the right kind of pen, an appropriate type of paper, and a good sense of humor.

13c To Introduce a Quotation

Use a colon to introduce a quotation.

Mark Twain made an interesting comment about dying: "Everyone wants to go to heaven, but no one wants to die."

211

13d Common Uses

Use a colon after the greeting in a formal business letter.

> Dear Sir or Madam:
> Dear Mr. Jones:
> To Whom It May Concern:

Use a colon to introduce the subtitle for a book or an article.

> BOOK   *Writing: Self-Expression and Communication*
>
> ARTICLE   "Ethics in America: Six Case Studies"

Use a colon to indicate time.

> 1:00 p.m.
> 7:15 a.m.

13e

Use a colon to indicate ratios and odds.

> 5:6 ratio
> odds of 2:1

Use a colon to separate the city of publication and the publisher of a book listed in a bibliography.

> Hawking, Stephen W. *A Brief History of Time*. Toronto: Bantam, 1988.

For more examples of colons used in bibliographies, see section 22h.

13e Common Errors

Do not use a colon to separate a verb and its objects.

INCORRECT The types of songs included in that collection are:
classical, easy listening, and jazz.

A colon in a sentence must have an independent clause before it.
The word group before *are* is not an independent clause, so no
punctuation is needed after *are*.

CORRECT The types of songs included in that collection are
classical, easy listening, and jazz.

Do not use a colon to separate an independent clause from
a dependent clause.

INCORRECT Although ethics means moral behavior to some
people: it means integrity to other people.

As stated earlier, a colon must have an independent clause before
it. The correct punctuation between a dependent clause and an
independent clause is a comma.

CORRECT Although ethics means moral behavior to some people, it means integrity to other people.

13e

■ A Student Writes

After several class discussions on the use of colons, Amy
Wolz's instructor had the class review their paragraphs on politics
for correct use of colons.

AMY'S PARAGRAPH

Most people think that politics are in federal, state, and local
government and nowhere else. They don't realize that politics
are: in families, on the job, at school, in relationships, and practically everywhere. Politics: means who gets what, when, where,
and how. In fact, politics can have any number of meanings.
Who gets the last donut in a box, who gets promoted first, who
gets to sit near the window in the classroom, and who gets the
last word in an argument. Thinking of politics on the government level is: merely scratching the surface of a really complex
issue.

Amy did not understand how to use colons, and she knew that she needed someone to look at her writing to see whether she had used them correctly. She asked her classmate Stephen to read her paragraph and answer the questions on the handout provided by the instructor.

◪ A Classmate Responds

QUESTIONS FOR REVIEW

1. Do the sentences with colons have an independent clause before the colon? Which ones do not?
2. Do any sentences have lists that need to be introduced with a colon? Which ones?

Stephen's answers were clear and informative.

STEPHEN'S RESPONSES

1. Sentences 2, 3, and 6. You have a colon right after or before a verb in those sentences, and they don't sound right.
2. Sentence 5 isn't really a sentence. It needs to be added to the sentence before it.

■ A Student Writes

Amy reread chapter 13 to review the use of colons. She then revised her paragraph.

AMY'S REVISED PARAGRAPH

Most people think that politics are in federal, state, and local government and nowhere else. They don't realize that politics are in families, on the job, at school, in relationships, and practically everywhere. Politics means who gets what, when, where, and how. In fact, politics can have any number of meanings: who gets the last donut in a box, who gets promoted first, who gets to sit near the window in the classroom, and who gets the last word in an argument. Thinking of politics on the government level is merely scratching the surface of a really complex issue.

Chapter 14

Apostrophes [']

14a Possessive Nouns and Pronouns

Use an apostrophe to indicate possessive nouns.

SINGULAR:	PLURAL:
APOSTROPHE + S	APOSTROPHE ONLY
John's guitar	the girls' pool
Mary's house	the boys' tent
Harris's ranch	the planets' sun

Notice that nouns that indicate plurals with an -s have only an apostrophe *after* the -s. Irregular noun plurals take an apostrophe with the -s.

IRREGULAR NOUN PLURALS

children's toys
fish's food
deer's antlers
people's ideas

Possessive personal pronouns do not have an apostrophe.

his	yours
hers	theirs
its	ours
whose	mine

14b Possessive Indefinite Pronouns

Use an apostrophe and an -*s* to indicate possessive indefinite pronouns.

everyone's sympathy
someone else's clock
someone's suggestion

14c Contractions

Use an apostrophe to indicate omitted letters in contractions.

I'm	I am
I've	I have
you're	you are
it's	it is
can't	cannot
don't	do not
doesn't	does not

14d

14d Plurals

Use an apostrophe and -*s* to indicate plurals of letters. No apostrophe is used for the plurals of numbers, years, and abbreviations.

P's and Q's	1990s
4s, fours	SATs

14e Common Errors

Do not use an apostrophe to indicate noun plurals.

INCORRECT The team of *dog's* was strong enough to pull the sled loaded with supplies.

CORRECT The team of *dogs* was strong enough to pull the sled loaded with supplies.

Do not use an apostrophe to indicate possessive personal pronouns.

INCORRECT The deer sheds *it's* antlers each year.

Since the contraction *it's* means *it is,* this sentence is illogical. The correct word is the possessive *its.*

CORRECT The deer sheds *its* antlers each year.

Also distinguish between *whose* and *who's.*

INCORRECT *Who's* books are these?

Since the contraction *who's* means *who is,* this sentence is illogical.

CORRECT *Whose* books are these?

14e

■ A Student Writes

After several class discussions on the use of apostrophes, Eric Schrader's instructor had the class review their paragraphs on being a college student for the correct use of apostrophes in possessives and contractions.

ERIC'S PARAGRAPH

   Juggling school and work is a challenge for most college student's today. Anyone who has to do both knows that an instructors demands are often similar to a supervisors demands. They
both want punctuality, long hours, and hard work. One problem
is a time conflict. The job sometimes ends almost at the same
time that the class begins, or vice versa. Another problem is that
the instructor expects a lot of time-consuming work (reading and
homework) done outside class. Sometimes, the instructors expectations interfere with the supervisors. Its hard for students
to know which one to please when they cant please both. The
solution to the problem may be to talk with the instructor as well
as the supervisor to explain the situation and to allow them to
offer suggestions.

   Since Eric wasn't sure how to use apostrophes, he asked
his classmate Caroline to look over his paragraph. Caroline used
the questions on the instructor's handout to check Eric's paragraph for apostrophe usage.

 ## A Classmate Responds

QUESTIONS FOR REVIEW

1. Do any contractions need apostrophes? In which sentences?
2. Do any words that show ownership (possession) need
   apostrophes? In which sentences?
3. Do any words have unnecessary apostrophes? In which
   sentences?

   Although Caroline's answers did not indicate which specific words needed apostrophes, her responses did help Eric locate his mistakes.

CAROLINE'S RESPONSES

1. Yes, sentence 7.
2. Yes, sentence 2 and sentence 6.
3. Yes, sentence 1.

■ A Student Writes

Eric reviewed chapter 14 and made the corrections for apostrophe usage in his paragraph.

ERIC'S REVISED PARAGRAPH

Juggling school and work is a challenge for most college students today. Anyone who has to do both knows that an instructor's demands are often similar to a supervisor's demands. They both want punctuality, long hours, and hard work. One problem is a time conflict. The job sometimes ends almost at the same time that the class begins, or vice versa. Another problem is that the instructor expects a lot of time-consuming work (reading and homework) done outside class. Sometimes, the instructor's expectations interfere with the supervisor's. It's hard for students to know which one to please when they can't please both. The solution to the problem may be to talk with the instructor as well as the supervisor to explain the situation and to allow them to offer suggestions.

Chapter 15

Quotation Marks [" "]

15a Direct Quotations

Use quotation marks to indicate a direct quotation.

John eventually stated the obvious: "I won the race!"

"Sunrise on the mountain," he said, "is simply breathtaking."

If a quotation is four lines or longer, it is usually indented from the rest of the text and quotation marks are omitted. See section 23b-2 for further explanation.

An indirect quotation, which reports what someone has said without repeating it word for word, should not be enclosed in quotation marks.

He said that sunrise on the mountain can take your breath away.

15b Quotations within Quotations

Use both double (" ") and single (' ') quotation marks to indicate a quotation or title within a quotation.

Sammy told the class, "Mark Twain said, 'Everyone wants to go to heaven, but no one wants to die.'"

15c Titles

Use quotation marks to indicate, within a piece of writing, the titles of articles, stories, poems, and songs.

NEWSPAPER ARTICLE "Animal Rights in America"

SHORT STORY "The Gift of the Magi" by O. Henry

POEM "The Charge of the Light Brigade" by Alfred Lord Tennyson

SONG "Shiny, Happy People" by R.E.M.

Do not use quotation marks around the title of your own essay when it is at the top of your paper.

15d With Other Punctuation Marks

15d

When using quotation marks, put commas and periods *inside* the quotation marks.

"Sunrise on the mountain," he said, "is simply breathtaking."

Colons and semicolons belong *outside* the quotation marks.

Sally agreed that "television advertising stimulates people to buy"; however, she did not agree that television advertising should be banned.

Question marks and exclamation points belong *inside* the quotation marks if they are part of the quotation. If they are used simply to end the sentence and are not part of the quotation, they belong *outside* the quotation marks.

Only the most sincere will ask, "What can I do to end the needless slaughter of animals?"

How many people under 30 have ever heard the song "Purple People Eater"?

■ A Student Writes

Each student in Jeff Townsend's composition class exchanged his or her paragraph with a classmate, who checked to see whether quotation marks were used correctly in titles and direct quotations.

JEFF'S PARAGRAPH

Adults are usually reluctant to admit that they play with their children's toys. Either they say, I am just showing my son how to use this, or they say, I am testing the toy to see if it works. I read an article recently called Nintendo Fever in Adults, which I thought clearly illustrated the fear some adults have of "being discovered". The article explained that many adults are closet Nintendo players. They love to play the game yet do not want other adults to know and make fun of them. These Nintendo addicts play the games after their children are at school or asleep at night, and they spend hours either trying to help the Mario Brothers save Yoshi and the Princess or trying to find Zelda's treasure. These adults choose, however, to keep their playing habits to themselves rather than risk ridicule from their peers. What they don't realize is that the people they fear telling are probably the biggest Nintendo fans of all.

15d

Jeff's classmate Craig looked over Jeff's draft and answered the questions on the handout provided by the instructor.

◤ A Classmate Responds

QUESTIONS FOR REVIEW

1. Do any sentences include titles that need to be enclosed with quotation marks? Which ones?
2. Is there any scrambled punctuation? For example, are there any periods outside quotation marks that should be inside them? Any colons inside quotation marks? Where?

3. Do any sentences have direct quotations but no quotation marks? Which ones? Are there quotation marks around any indirect quotations that need to be removed? Where?

Craig's responses made Jeff realize that the correct use of quotation marks can dramatically improve the readability of a piece of writing.

CRAIG'S RESPONSES

1. Sentence 3.
2. At the end of the same sentence.
3. Sentence 2 is confusing. I think you need to put quotation marks around the I statements. Don't forget that the comma and the period both go inside the quotation marks.

■ A Student Writes

Jeff used Craig's responses to correct his paragraph.

JEFF'S REVISED PARAGRAPH

Adults are usually reluctant to admit that they play with their children's toys. Either they say, "I am just showing my son how to use this," or they say, "I am testing the toy to see if it works." I read an article recently called "Nintendo Fever in Adults," which I thought clearly illustrated the fear some adults have of "being discovered." The article explained that many adults are closet Nintendo players. They love to play the game yet do not want other adults to know and make fun of them. These Nintendo addicts play the games after their children are at school or asleep at night, and they spend hours either trying to help the Mario Brothers save Yoshi and the Princess or trying to find Zelda's treasure. These adults choose, however, to keep their playing habits to themselves rather than risk ridicule from their peers. What they don't realize is that the people they fear telling are probably the biggest Nintendo fans of all.

Chapter 16

End Punctuation

16a Periods [.]

Use a period at the end of a sentence.

The end of the semester is a difficult time for a lot of students. Sometimes, students have to write term papers and study for final exams.

16b Question Marks [?]

Use a question mark when asking a direct question.

When do the swallows return to Capistrano?

Be careful not to use a question mark for an indirect question — when the sentence refers to or reports a question.

> INCORRECT I often wonder why the Midwest summer nights are so tranquil?

This sentence has an independent clause (*I often wonder*) and a dependent clause (*why the Midwest summer nights are so tranquil*). Because the sentence is referring to a question rather than actually asking a question, the correct punctuation is a period.

> CORRECT I often wonder why the Midwest summer nights are so tranquil.

225

16c Exclamation Points [!]

Use an exclamation point to emphasize, to express strong emotion, or to attract attention.

Wow! Susan just won the tennis match!

Go home!

Help!

Be careful to use exclamation points sparingly, or they will lose their impact.

■ A Student Writes

After several class discussions on the use of end punctuation, Hermina Mugamba's instructor had the class review a paragraph of their choice. The purpose of the review was to check for the correct use of end punctuation.

HERMINA'S PARAGRAPH

One of the biggest mistakes I ever made was to invite one of my classmates to study at my house. We were going to spend a few hours one afternoon studying for an algebra test we weren't sure where a quiet place would be, so I suggested my house. She asked if she could bring her little seven-year-old, she said she was quiet, well behaved, and no trouble. What she didn't tell me was that her little seven-year-old was a cantankerous old Siamese cat, that cat was not quiet or well behaved and was more trouble than it was worth the next time someone wants to visit with a "little one," I plan to ask what species?

Hermina felt that her punctuation was awkward. So she asked her classmate Matthew to read her paragraph and answer the questions on the instructor's handout.

☑ A Classmate Responds

QUESTIONS FOR REVIEW

1. When read aloud slowly, do any sentences sound or look like two independent clauses that need to be separated with a period? Which ones?
2. Do any sentences sound or look like two independent clauses connected with a comma? Which ones?
3. Do any sentences use the wrong form of end punctuation? Which ones?

Matthew's answers showed Hermina that she needed to study chapter 16 to learn how to use end punctuation correctly.

MATTHEW'S RESPONSES

1. Sentence 2 runs together two sentences that need to be separated with a period.
2. Sentence 3 does. And sentence 4 sounds like several sentences all crammed together.
3. I don't think the last sentence should have a question mark.

■ A Student Writes

Hermina used Matthew's comments and suggestions to correct her paragraph after she reviewed chapter 16.

HERMINA'S REVISED PARAGRAPH

One of the biggest mistakes I ever made was to invite one of my classmates to study at my house. We were going to spend a few hours one afternoon studying for an algebra test. We weren't sure where a quiet place would be, so I suggested my house. She asked if she could bring her little seven-year-old. She said she was quiet, well behaved, and no trouble. What she didn't tell me was that her little seven-year-old was a cantankerous old Siamese cat. That cat was not quiet or well behaved and was more trouble than it was worth. The next time someone wants to visit with a "little one," I plan to ask what species.

Chapter 17

Other Punctuation Marks

17a Hyphen [-]

Use a hyphen to combine numbers written as words.

> forty-one   seven-tenths

Use a hyphen to connect words in compound expressions.

> mother-in-law   father-in-law

Use a hyphen to connect words that function as one modifier of a noun.

> second-class citizen
> middle-class person
> nineteenth-century writer

Use a hyphen to connect the prefixes *self-* and *all-* to words.

Some people easily become self-sufficient.

The meaning of that word is all-inclusive.

Use a hyphen to connect any prefix to a proper noun.

The temperature in mid-July is almost unbearable.

Use a hyphen to indicate the syllable divisions in a word at the end of a line.

Sam gave Janie a horse for her birthday because he understood how much she wanted one.

Campers can have great fun in the outdoors when conditions are favorable.

If you are unsure where to divide a word with a hyphen, check the dictionary.

17b Dash [—]

Dashes emphasize the elements they enclose and set them off from the rest of the sentence.
Use a dash like a colon to set off a list.

The doberman will eat just about anything — fingers, toes, whatever he wants.

Use a dash to separate an example, an explanation, or an illustration from the rest of the sentence.

The husky — all 85 pounds of her — loves children.

A dash is *not* a hyphen, but it is indicated by typing or writing two hyphens (--) with no spaces to the left or right of the hyphens.

17c Parentheses [( )]

Use parentheses to separate information — an example, an explanation, an illustration, nonrestrictive modifiers, and the like — from the rest of the sentence. Parentheses enclose information that would otherwise interrupt the sentence.

Jack (who really wants to remain anonymous) donated a month's salary to the American Cancer Society.

Campers need certain equipment (a tent, a sleeping bag, a stove, and a lantern) to make camping enjoyable.

If the parentheses are at the end of the sentence, the end punctuation belongs outside the parentheses.

Campers need certain equipment (a tent, a sleeping bag, a stove, and a lantern).

If an entire sentence is in parentheses, the end punctuation belongs inside the parentheses.

The temperature in Whitehorse today is 85 degrees. (The Yukon is not known for such extreme heat.)

17d Brackets [ ]

Use brackets to indicate an explanation of or an addition to a direct quotation.

Walking to the helicopter, the President explained, "He [Jack Jones] was an excellent politician."

The bracketed information gives the reader the name of the person, which is needed for a clear reading of the sentence. Otherwise, the reader would not know who *He* is.

In the next example the bracketed information tells readers the quantity of the snowfall.

"This year," said the meteorologist, "the city of Chicago has had less snowfall [only 15 inches] than in any previous year."

Use brackets to indicate parentheses inside of parentheses.

In a math problem (such as $2[x + 3y] + [x + y]$), do the multiplication before the addition.

17d

17e   Ellipsis Periods [. . .]

Use three ellipsis periods to indicate an omission in a direct quotation.

ORIGINAL

Jackson explains that "when water reaches a certain level, what appears to be a point of no return, it will eventually taper off."

WITH ELLIPSIS

Jackson explains that "when water reaches a certain level . . . it will eventually taper off."

If the ellipsis periods are at the end of the sentence, be sure to add another period to indicate the end punctuation.

Hamlet's most famous speech is "To be, or not to be. . . ."

17f

17f   Slash [/]

Use the slash to separate dates and alternative words.

5/5/94
and/or

■   A Student Writes

After a class discussion of the various types of punctuation marks, Le Quan Su's instructor had the class check their paragraphs on career choices for the correct use of punctuation.

LE QUAN'S PARAGRAPH

When I began to think of a career choice, I first thought maybe I wanted to become some type of health care professional. Nursing was a possibility, but physical therapy sounded more intriguing. Both careers pay well, but what I really wanted was something challenging that involved children. Eventually, I decided on pediatric physical therapy because I felt there would be more one on one contact with patients. Although nurses do have a lot of personal contact with their patients, physical therapists have more. They are right there with one patient for several hours at a time, working with the patient to develop, strengthen, or retrain muscles. As far as I'm concerned, the intense one on one relationship that physical therapists have with patients makes the job fulfilling.

Le Quan asked her classmate Mike to read her paragraph and answer the questions about punctuation on the handout provided by the instructor.

◢ A Classmate Responds

QUESTIONS FOR REVIEW

1. Do any sentences have combined words used as modifiers that need hyphens? Which ones? *Hint:* Look at the words in front of nouns.
2. Do any sentences use hyphens that should be dashes? Which ones?

Mike's answers helped Le Quan decide which changes she needed to make.

MIKE'S RESPONSES

1. In the sentence that starts with "Eventually" and in the last sentence, "one on one" needs hyphens.
2. No, there are no hyphens.

■ A Student Writes

Le Quan used Mike's suggestions to correct her paragraph.

LE QUAN'S REVISED PARAGRAPH

When I began to think of a career choice, I first thought maybe I wanted to become some type of health care professional. Nursing was a possibility, but physical therapy sounded more intriguing. Both careers pay well, but what I really wanted was something challenging that involved children. Eventually, I decided on pediatric physical therapy because I felt there would be more one-on-one contact with patients. Although nurses do have a lot of personal contact with their patients, physical therapists have more. They are right there with one patient for several hours at a time, working with the patient to develop, strengthen, or retrain muscles. As far as I'm concerned, the intense one-on-one relationship that physical therapists have with patients makes the job fulfilling.

Chapter 18

Italics
(Underlining)

18a Titles

Use underlining to indicate italics (a slanted typeface used in printed text) for titles of books, magazines, newspapers, pamphlets, movies, videos, television shows, albums, plays, and long poems.

BOOKS <u>The Prince and the Pauper</u>

MAGAZINES <u>Time</u>   <u>Newsweek</u>

NEWSPAPERS <u>The New York Times</u>

PAMPHLETS <u>A Modest Proposal</u>

MOVIES <u>Hook</u>   <u>Fantasia</u>

VIDEOS <u>Aerobics Workout</u>

TELEVISION SHOWS <u>Northern Exposure</u>

ALBUMS <u>Sgt. Pepper's Lonely Hearts Club Band</u>

PLAYS <u>Hamlet</u>   <u>Romeo and Juliet</u>

LONG POEMS <u>In Memoriam A. H. H.</u>

18b Foreign Words

Underline foreign words and phrases that have not become accepted as part of the English language.

Years ago, certain textbooks contained an <u>imprimatur</u>, which literally means "let it be printed."

18c To Emphasize Words as Words

Use underlining to emphasize a word as a word.

Writers can use <u>you</u> when they have a close relationship with their readers.

The spelling of <u>weird</u> is confusing and seems to contradict the rule about using <u>i</u> before <u>e</u>.

18d

18d Common Errors

Do not use underlining very often for emphasis because it can become distracting to the reader as well as create a breathless tone.

INCORRECT

The debate <u>was</u> meant to be <u>dynamic</u>, and the audience applauded <u>very</u> loudly after the debaters' <u>incredible</u> rebuttal.

To correct this sentence, eliminate the underlining entirely.

■ A Student Writes

After a class discussion on the use of underlining (italics), Lisa Rae's instructor had the class review their paragraphs on the circus for the correct use of underlining.

LISA'S PARAGRAPH

I have always enjoyed going to the circus. Some of my fondest childhood memories are of visiting the Ringling Brothers Circus and the Barnum and Bailey Circus. I always thought a circus had to have animals. However, after reading an article in Time magazine several years ago, I became familiar with a different type of circus—one without animals. Cirque du Soleil is the name of a troop of French Canadians (from Montreal) who have developed a unique type of circus. The "Circus of the Stars," as they call themselves, specializes in a combination of traditional acrobats, high-wire acts, and clowns, as well as nontraditional ballet dancers, modern dancers, and new-wave music. A common theme permeates all the acts, and everything is perfectly choreographed and "finished"—even the trapeze artists' descent to the net and exit. The music is unlike any used in traditional circuses. In fact, when I had the opportunity to see Cirque du Soleil, I was amazed at how the music reflected not only the meaning of each particular act but also the enthusiasm of the performers. Each year, the troop takes a new show across Canada and the United States. Their 1992 show was called Nouvelle Experience—"a new experience"—and the 1993 show is entitled Saltimbanco—"the trickster." This circus is an innovative and exhilarating event that should not be missed.

Lisa asked her classmate Derek to read her paragraph and answer the questions on the instructor's handout.

◤ A Classmate Responds

QUESTIONS FOR REVIEW

1. Do any sentences have titles that need to be underlined? Which ones?

2. Do any sentences have foreign words that need to be underlined? Which ones?

Derek's answers gave Lisa some suggestions about changes she needed to make in her draft.

DEREK'S RESPONSES

1. Sentence 4 has the name of a magazine.
2. Sentences 5, 9, and 11 all have foreign words.

■ A Student Writes

Lisa used Derek's suggestions to correct her paragraph.

LISA'S REVISED PARAGRAPH

I have always enjoyed going to the circus. Some of my fondest childhood memories are of visiting the Ringling Brothers Circus and the Barnum and Bailey Circus. I always thought a circus had to have animals. However, after reading an article in <u>Time</u> magazine several years ago, I became familiar with a different type of circus — one without animals. <u>Cirque du Soleil</u> is the name of a troop of French Canadians (from Montreal) who have developed a unique type of circus. The "Circus of the Stars," as they call themselves, specializes in a combination of traditional acrobats, high-wire acts, and clowns, as well as nontraditional ballet dancers, modern dancers, and new-wave music. A common theme permeates all the acts, and everything is perfectly choreographed and "finished" — even the trapeze artists' descent to the net and exit. The music is unlike any used in traditional circuses. In fact, when I had the opportunity to see <u>Cirque du Soleil</u>, I was amazed at how the music reflected not only the meaning of each particular act but also the enthusiasm of the performers. Each year, the troop takes a new show across Canada and the United States. Their 1992 show was called <u>Nouvelle Experience</u> — "a new experience" — and the 1993 show is entitled <u>Saltimbanco</u> — "the trickster." This circus is an innovative and exhilarating event that should not be missed.

Chapter 19

Numbers and Abbreviations

19a Spelling Out Numbers

Generally, numbers under 10 should be spelled out.

A presidential term lasts only four years.

Numbers of 10 and over should be indicated with numerals unless the number begins the sentence.

Every 15 minutes, the clock in the hall chimes.

Forty people signed the petition.

When several numbers are used in a sentence, be consistent: spell them all out, or use numerals, for all of them.

INCORRECT

On election day one out of 9 people voted yes for recycling.

The chances are 50 to seven that she will win the game.

CORRECT

On election day one out of nine people voted yes for recycling. [Spell out all numbers, since all are under 10.]

The chances are 50 to 7 that she will win the game. [Use all numerals in a sentence when some numbers should be spelled out and some should be numerals.]

OR The chances are 50:7 that she will win the game.

19b Using Numerals

Numerals are usually acceptable for dates, addresses, money, percentages, divisions of books and plays, pagination, time, fractions and decimals, ratios, scores, and statistics.

DATES 6 November 1991   AD 2   4 BC

ADDRESSES

2401 South Walnut Street, Apt. 4

Southwest 2nd Avenue

MONEY $2.32 $.72

PERCENTAGES 86%   .01%   2%

DIVISIONS OF BOOKS/PLAYS

volume 6   chapter 2   act II, scene 4

PAGINATION p. 2   pp. 4–7

TIME 3:04   12:00 noon

FRACTIONS AND DECIMALS ¾   3.14

RATIOS 2:4   30:1

SCORES 7–10   11 to 4

STATISTICS

6 out of every 8 people   the average height is 6′ 11″

19c Abbreviations

Abbreviations are useful when you refer to people with titles and to organizations, phrases, degrees, and time if those names are long and distracting to the reader. However, use an abbreviation only after the full name has first been identified.

TITLES WITH PROPER NAMES

Mr. Thomas Jefferson
Mrs. Dolly Madison
Martin Luther King, Jr.
Dr. Margaret Denny
Ms. Lisa Wilson

ORGANIZATIONS, CORPORATIONS, COUNTRIES

ABC	American Broadcasting Company
CIA	Central Intelligence Agency
NABISCO	National Biscuit Company
USA	United States of America

COMMON ABBREVIATIONS

AD	*anno Domini*, "in the year of the Lord" (AD 24)
am	amplitude modulation (radio stations)
a.m.	ante meridian (morning)
BC	before Christ (14 BC)
bldg.	building
EST	eastern standard time
fm	frequency modulation (radio stations)
lb.	pound
lbs.	pounds
min.	minute
mins.	minutes
no.	number
oz.	ounce, ounces
p.	page
p.m.	post meridian (afternoon)
pp.	pages
PS	post script
sec.	second
secs.	seconds

19c

NAMES OF DEGREES

AA	Associate of Arts
BA	Bachelor of Arts
D.D.S.	Doctor of Dental Surgery
D.V.M.	Doctor of Veterinary Medicine

EdD	Doctor of Education
L.P.N.	licensed practical nurse
MA	Master of Arts
PhD	Doctor of Philosophy
R.N.	registered nurse

NAMES OF MONTHS (in bibliographic entries)

Jan.	January
Feb.	February
Mar.	March

LATIN ABBREVIATIONS

e.g.	*exempli gratia,* "for example"
et al.	*et alia,* "and others"
etc.	*et cetera,* "and so on"
i.e.	*id est,* "that is"
NB	*nota bene,* "note well"
viz.	*videlicet,* "namely"

19d

19d Inappropriate Abbreviations

Avoid the overuse of abbreviations in formal writing. Usually, proper names, units of measurements, months, days of the week, holidays, states, and countries should be written out rather than abbreviated.

ACCEPTED	NOT ACCEPTED
William	Wm.
ounce	oz. (except in natural science writing)
January	Jan. (except in some bibliography entries)
Monday	Mon.
Christmas	Xmas
Illinois	Ill. or IL (except in some bibliography entries)
Germany	Ger.

■ A Student Writes

After a class discussion on how to use numbers and abbreviations, Juan Carrera's instructor had the class review a paragraph of their choice for the correct use of numbers and abbreviations.

JUAN'S PARAGRAPH

2 times a year, we are treated to an adventure in physics. Once in the spring and again in the fall, we are in the midst of the equinox. The term equinox means "equal night," and for 1 day in the spring and one day in the fall, the number of daylight hours equals the number of nighttime hours. The spring, or vernal, equinox falls on the 1st day of spring in Mar.; and the fall, or autumnal, equinox falls on the 1st day of autumn in Sept. Because on these 2 days the earth is equidistant from the sun and the moon, the gravitational pull from each is equal. This change in gravity gives people a chance to perform a common stunt on these 2 days — egg balancing. Because of the equal gravitational pull, a person can balance a raw egg on end on a level surface. Usually, at least one person will appear on a local news station grinning because of his or her success with such a trick.

Juan asked his classmate Brian to review his paragraph for the use of numbers and abbreviations.

☑ A Classmate Responds

QUESTIONS FOR REVIEW

1. Do any sentences begin with numerals instead of numbers spelled out? Which ones?
2. Do any sentences have both numerals and numbers spelled out? Which ones?
3. Do any sentences have numerals that need to be spelled out? Which ones?
4. Do any sentences have abbreviations when the whole word should be used instead? Which ones?

Brian's answers helped Juan see the corrections he needed to make in his paragraph.

BRIAN'S RESPONSES

1. The first one.
2. The sentence that begins with "The term" uses both.
3. Sentence 5 and sentence 6 have numbers under 10.
4. Sentence 4 has abbreviations for months and for 1st that I think are not acceptable.

■ A Student Writes

Juan read Brian's answers and used the comments to correct his paragraph.

JUAN'S REVISED PARAGRAPH

Two times a year, we are treated to an adventure in physics. Once in the spring and again in the fall, we are in the midst of the equinox. The term equinox means "equal night," and for one day in the spring and one day in the fall, the number of daylight hours equals the number of nighttime hours. The spring, or vernal, equinox falls on the first day of spring in March; and the fall, or autumnal, equinox falls on the first day of autumn in September. Because on these two days the earth is equidistant from the sun and the moon, the gravitational pull from each is equal. This change in gravity gives people a chance to perform a common stunt on these two days — egg balancing. Because of the equal gravitational pull, a person can balance a raw egg on end on a level surface. Usually, at least one person will appear on a local news station grinning because of his or her success with such a trick.

Chapter 20

Capitalization

20a First Word in a Sentence

Use a capital letter to begin the first word in every sentence.

*T*hose seal pups at the zoo are beautiful.

20b First Word in a Quoted Sentence

Use a capital letter to begin the first word in a quotation that is an independent clause.

According to Tom's neighbors, "*E*veryone in the neighborhood wants to be responsible for recycling trash."

"*T*he outdoors in the winter is a camper's dream," explained the half-frozen camper, "but sometimes that dream is a frosty one."

20c Titles of Works

Use capital letters for the important words (usually not prepositions or articles) in titles of articles, books, songs, poems, and other works.

"The Fine Points of Academic Freedom"

The Prince and the Pauper by Mark Twain

"Sailing on the Tide"

PUBLICATIONS AND MOVIES

Books

The American Heritage Dictionary
Biomedical Ethics

Magazines

Time
Newsweek

Newspapers

The New York Times
The Wall Street Journal

Movies

The War of the Roses
The Wizard of Oz

20d Proper vs. Common Nouns

Use capital letters for proper nouns (nouns that name a specific person, place, or thing) and adjectives made from proper nouns (the adjective *Jewish,* which comes from the noun *Jew*). The following lists illustrate examples of proper nouns and proper adjectives that are capitalized regardless of where they appear in a sentence.

NAMES Mary Jones   Bob Smith

NATIONALITIES

American
Russian
Chinese

RACES AND RELIGIONS

African-American
American-Eskimo
Jewish

RELATIVES

Uncle Bill   (but not in *my uncle*)
Mom   (but not in *my mom*)
Dad   (but not in *my dad*)

TITLES

Dr. Smith
President Lincoln
Vice President Jones

LOCATIONS

Europe   Sussex County
Japan   Belmont Road
Idaho   Route 66
Toronto   Lake Ontario

20d

BUSINESSES, ORGANIZATIONS, AND CHURCHES

McDonald's   Library of Congress
General Motors   St. Joseph Hospital
National Organization for Women   New Christian Church
Union Club   Yale University

SPECIFIC SCHOOL COURSES

Biology 101   Geometry 306
Physics 115   Chemistry 201

However, when you refer to a school subject in general, do not capitalize the name of the subject unless another rule requires you to do so.

Someday, Sandy will find that her background in geometry and French will be very helpful.

LANGUAGES

English   Greek
French   Latin

SPECIFIC SEASONS AND HOLIDAYS

Fall 1989   Memorial Day
Spring 1978   Veterans Day
Winter 1985   Yom Kippur

Do not capitalize seasons of the year (*in the fall*) unless the year follows.

MONTHS AND DAYS January   Friday

HISTORICAL EVENTS, DOCUMENTS, AND ACTS

Civil War   Boston Tea Party
Constitution of the United States   First Amendment

LANDMARKS AND STRUCTURES

Statue of Liberty   Leaning Tower of Pisa
the White House   Empire State Building

MAJOR SPORTS EVENTS

Kentucky Derby   World Series

20e

20e Letter Greetings and Closings

Use capital letters for the words in letter greetings and closings.

Dear Sir:
Dear Madam:
To Whom It May Concern:
Sincerely,
Yours truly,

Notice that only the first word in a closing is capitalized.

20f *I* and *O*

Always use a capital letter for the personal pronoun *I*.

> After much thought, I decided to work overtime yesterday.

Always use a capital letter for the poetic comment *O*.

> As I let my mind wander, I remembered: O how lovely is the fall.

■ A Student Writes

After a class discussion on capitalization, Angela Cardinals's instructor had the class review their paragraphs on their favorite city. They were to check for the correct use of capital letters.

ANGELA'S PARAGRAPH

My favorite city is Chicago, which is the home of the Chicago cubs baseball team. I like Chicago for its size, its Museums, its lakefront areas, its restaurants, and its excitement. the city is large, but it is not so large that you have trouble finding what you need. For example, if i need to find a particular Museum or restaurant, all i have to do is ask any bus driver or police officer for directions. Most of the people there are friendly and are eager to show off their city. the excitement of Chicago is incredible. There are many events and activities to participate in during the day, and there are always plays, operas, concerts, and other events to indulge in at night. And, of course, Chicago is the home of the cubs — the greatest american baseball team i know.

Angela's classmate Christina read her paragraph and answered the questions on the handout provided by the instructor.

◩ A Classmate Responds

1. Do all sentences begin with capital letters?
2. Do any sentences have proper nouns or adjectives that need to be capitalized? Which ones?
3. Are any words capitalized that shouldn't be? Which ones?
4. Is the word *I* capitalized in all places?

Christina's answers showed Angela that she needed to make a few corrections in her paragraph.

1. No, some don't.
2. The first and the last sentence.
3. <u>Museums</u> in sentence 2 and <u>Museum</u> in sentence 4.
4. Not in the last sentence.

■ A Student Writes

Angela reread her paragraph and she caught one problem that Christina hadn't seen. In addition to capitalizing the *i* in the last sentence, she capitalized the *i*'s in the fourth sentence.

My favorite city is Chicago, which is the home of the Chicago Cubs baseball team. I like Chicago for its size, its museums, its lakefront areas, its restaurants, and its excitement. The city is large, but it is not so large that you have trouble finding what you need. For example, if I need to find a particular museum or restaurant, all I have to do is ask any bus driver or police officer for directions. Most of the people there are friendly and are eager to show off their city. The excitement of Chicago is incredible. There are many events and activities to participate in during the day, and there are always plays, operas, concerts, and other events to indulge in at night. And, of course, Chicago is the home of the Cubs — the greatest American baseball team I know.

Part 5

The Research-
Based Essay

Part 5   The Research-Based Essay

Chapter 21

Gathering Information

21a Deciding on a Topic

When you choose a topic for a research paper, you should select a question or an idea that interests you, that relates to the course requiring the paper, that is appropriate for the audience and purpose of the assignment, and that can be researched in the time given. Often the instructor will provide several ideas for topics, and you will need to choose one and focus it. For example, in a music class your topic might be a choice of composers from a specific time period. In an English class you might have a choice of short story writers or characters in a short story; in a philosophy class, a choice of ethical problems; in a psychology class, a choice of behavioral problems.

Sometimes, before you begin to write about a particular topic or do library research, you need to gather ideas and opinions from various sources. This preliminary information will help you to put your initial ideas into perspective or to further narrow your topic.

This initial information gathering, or preliminary research, can be approached on several levels. For instance, you might look at preliminary research as idea gathering or idea and information sharing that gives you the opportunity to learn all sorts of fascinating information and to focus your thesis. Or you might approach preliminary research just as you would any situation in which you needed to get information. For example, when you have questions about everyday problems or questions about an issue in one of your courses, how do you find the answers? Usually, you ask someone who knows, or you do research to find the answers. These questioning techniques work just as well when you need information for writing.

21b Obtaining Preliminary Information

Some people have a routine that they always follow when they go to the library. First, they go straight to the card catalogue (or computer terminal) and look up books on their topic. Next, they choose a stack of these books at random, take them home, open them, and begin their search for information. There are other ways to use the library.

Many libraries now have computerized card catalogues that enable you to find a list of books on a topic very quickly. All you do is sit at a computer terminal and type in a subject, a title, or an author. The computer then lists all the available books along with their call numbers. (A call number tells you where the book is located in the library.)

When confronted in this manner with a lengthy list of books, you have to decide simply by looking at the title whether or not a particular book has information you can use. Selecting sources in this way is usually difficult and often ineffective. A better method for finding relevant information about your topic is to consult newspapers, encyclopedias, indexes, and other reference works, as discussed in the rest of this chapter. Such reference works will lead you to specific books about your topic.

Because of the time involved in publishing books, the information in most books is at least a year out of date by the time it is published. So if your topic depends on up-to-date information, check the facts in the books you are using against facts given in current sources, like recent issues of magazines and journals.

21b-1 Read Newspapers

Try reading newspapers for current information on a topic. Newspapers can provide interesting and usually dependable information on a wide range of current topics. For instance, if the topic is a current election, check the political sections of newspapers for ideas. If the topic is related to the status of a particular company, like IBM, check the business sections. However, you need to become a careful reader. While some newspapers are usually reliable, not everything in print is 100% accurate. For questions that will help you decide whether an article is a reliable source of information, see section 1a-9.

21b-2 Consult Encyclopedias

Sometimes, you may want to do some preliminary reading on a topic that you know little about or that you do not understand. One of the best sources for this kind of background information is an encyclopedia. The purpose of an encyclopedia article is to explain a topic in general terms and to make it interesting. Since encyclopedias have many different authors, they include a variety of opinions and approaches to topics.

Encyclopedias list information alphabetized by subject and provide easy access to information that is usually accurate and often valuable. The following regular encyclopedias are usually available in libraries.

> *Encyclopedia Americana*
> *Encyclopaedia Britannica*
> *World Book Encyclopedia*

Many libraries also have specialized encyclopedias.

> *Encyclopedia of Animal Behavior*
> *Encyclopedia of Popular Music*
> *Encyclopedia of Sports*
> *McGraw-Hill Encyclopedia of Science and Technology*

The information found in encyclopedias is useful for preliminary research. An encyclopedia, however, is not usually considered a source of information written by experts and, therefore, should not be cited as a source in an essay or referred to on a Works Cited or References page. Since the information included is general, encyclopedias can be used to find key words and to locate other sources of information on your topic.

21b

21b-3 Consult Almanacs and Atlases

Almanacs and atlases provide facts, figures, and a comprehensive overview of information and thus are valuable as preliminary reading. Since almanacs are usually updated and published annually, their information is relatively up to date. Atlases often combine geographical information with political, historical, and ecological information. For example, if you want to compare the average salary of a factory worker in Japan and the average salary of a factory worker in America, an almanac can provide you with the information. Likewise, if you want to find out where a particular country is located, you can consult an atlas. Libraries usually have the following popular and practical almanacs and atlases.

*Almanac of American
    Politics
Almanac of Famous People
Information Please
    Almanac: Atlas and
    Yearbook
Information Please
    Almanac: The New
    Universe of Information*

*World Almanac and Book
    of Facts
Hammond Ambassador
    World Atlas
New Rand McNally
    College World Atlas
Times Atlas of the World*

21b-4 Consult Dictionaries

21b

Dictionaries can also provide a wealth of information useful as background material. Dictionaries vary according to the kind of information presented in them. For example, unabridged dictionaries (like the *Oxford English Dictionary*) provide definitions of words in contemporary usage as well as definitions of archaic, rare, and obscure words. Collegiate dictionaries (like *The American Heritage Dictionary*) provide definitions of words commonly used. Etymological dictionaries (like the *Oxford Dictionary of Word Origins*) provide definitions as well as historical information on the origins and development of words. Biographical dictionaries (like the *Dictionary of American Biography*) provide information about the lives of significant people. Specialized dictionaries (like art, music, medical, and nursing dictionaries) provide information on terminology relevant to particular disciplines. Consult your instructor or a reference librarian to find out which dictionary would be most helpful to you.

21b-5 Interview People

Once you have done enough reading about your topic to ask informed questions, you can interview people who are specialists in your area of interest. You will want to select people who, because of their expertise, can give you reliable information. For example, let's say you are going to write about animal rights. You can interview people who belong to animal rights organizations and researchers on your campus who use animals in their experiments. Here are some typical questions you might ask.

1. Do you think animals should be used in medical experiments? Why or why not?
2. Do you think animals should be used to test products such as cosmetics? Why or why not?
3. Do you think animals should be raised for food? Why or why not?
4. What are the alternatives to using animals for these purposes? Is it absolutely necessary to use animals to test cosmetics, for example?
5. How should animals be treated? For example, do you think it is okay to raise animals used for food in crowded, unsanitary conditions? Is it okay to breed rats specifically for use in scientific experiments? Why or why not?
6. Who should be allowed to decide how animals used in experiments or raised for food should be treated? For example, should the government decide what is appropriate? Should individual people be able to choose?
7. Do you think that animals have the same basic rights as human beings? Why or why not?

21b

Before developing this list of questions, you would have gathered some preliminary information about the different ways animals are used — for medical experiments, for testing products, and, of course, for food — and identified some of the main issues that bothered you about the way animals are treated in these different situations. In this way you will be able to get specific information that you can use in your paper, instead of wasting your interview time asking basic questions.

21c   Deciding on Key Words

Doing preliminary research — consulting encyclopedias or almanacs, talking to experts — and talking to your instructor can help you find key words. **Key words** are words that are necessary for finding sources of information about your topic. In your reading you may notice that certain words or phrases are repeated in several different sources. Keep a record of these key words and phrases. They will help you as you begin to do more focused research on your topic. For example, in periodicals' indexes, discussed in section 21d, you can use key words to find lists of articles related to your topic.

The *Library of Congress Subject Headings* (*LCSH*) is another source of key words. Katie O'Sullivan, the student who wrote the research-based essay in section 23e, wanted to find information about the humane and inhumane treatment of animals. When Katie did not find listings for "humane treatment of animals," "inhumane treatment of animals," or "prevention of cruelty to animals" in any indexes or in the *LCSH*, she asked a reference librarian for help. The librarian thought of some possibilities that Katie hadn't considered, such as "animal rights movement" and "animal welfare," which led her to new sources of information.

When you already have some knowledge about your topic, brainstorming can provide some possible key words. For example, for the topic of cigarette advertising, you might brainstorm and produce the following list.

21c

BRAINSTORMING

stereotypes
layout
ad copy
hidden messages (subliminals)
cancer research
men in advertising
women in advertising
animals in advertising
surgeon general

As you search periodical indexes, you may have to rearrange your ideas to find further information. For the last three items in the brainstorming list, for example, you would first look under the general category "advertising" to find out about men, women, and animals used in advertising.

21d Using Indexes

To efficiently find information in magazines and journals, use an **index,** a listing (usually alphabetical) of articles printed within a certain year or month. Before using an index, though, create a list of key words (section 21c) to help in your search for information.

21d-1 *New York Times Index*

This source is an annual index to all the articles that have appeared in the *New York Times*. Articles are listed alphabetically by subject. A sample entry follows.

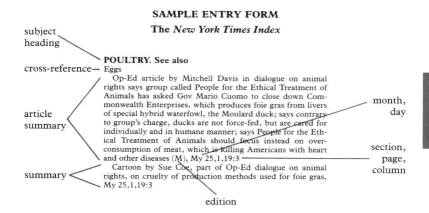

SAMPLE ENTRY FORM
The *New York Times Index*

subject heading

cross-reference—

POULTRY. See also
Eggs
Op-Ed article by Mitchell Davis in dialogue on animal rights says group called People for the Ethical Treatment of Animals has asked Gov Mario Cuomo to close down Commonwealth Enterprises, which produces foie gras from livers of special hybrid waterfowl, the Moulard duck; says contrary to group's charge, ducks are not force-fed, but are cared for individually and in humane manner; says People for the Ethical Treatment of Animals should focus instead on overconsumption of meat, which is killing Americans with heart and other diseases (M), My 25,1,19:3
Cartoon by Sue Coe, part of Op-Ed dialogue on animal rights, on cruelty of production methods used for foie gras, My 25,1,19:3

article summary

summary

month, day

section, page, column

edition

21d

This entry from the *New York Times* index gave Katie the name of an animal rights organization, People for the Ethical Treatment of Animals.

21d-2 *Readers' Guide to Periodical Literature*

You can find information in magazines and journals by using the *Readers' Guide to Periodical Literature*. For example, if you want to find current articles on health care, use your key words to look for entries in the *Readers' Guide*. This index will give you bibliographical information for specific articles listed under some of your key words. Included with the title of each article listed will be the information you need (author, title of magazine, volume number, page numbers, date) to help you find the actual article. You should keep an accurate record of this information for two reasons: (1) You can use the information to locate the article, and (2) later, you will use some of the information on the Works Cited page of your essay.

The *Readers' Guide* is an annual index to articles published in nonliterary periodicals such as *Time, Newsweek, Jet,* or *Psychology Today*. Articles are listed by subject headings arranged in alphabetical order, as shown in the following sample entry.

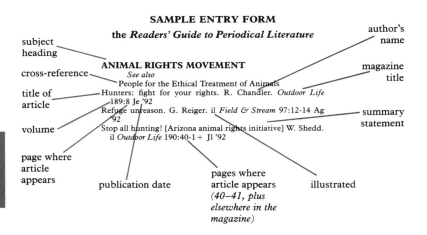

SAMPLE ENTRY FORM
the *Readers' Guide to Periodical Literature*

subject heading

cross-reference

title of article

volume

author's name

magazine title

ANIMAL RIGHTS MOVEMENT
     See also
People for the Ethical Treatment of Animals
Hunters: fight for your rights. R. Chandler. *Outdoor Life* 189:8 Je '92
Refuge unreason. G. Reiger. il *Field & Stream* 97:12-14 Ag '92
Stop all hunting! [Arizona animal rights initiative] W. Shedd. il *Outdoor Life* 190:40-1 + Jl '92

summary statement

page where article appears

publication date

pages where article appears (*40–41, plus elsewhere in the magazine*)

illustrated

21d

Notice that this entry shows that People for the Ethical Treatment of Animals has a separate entry in the *Readers' Guide*.

To find the article itself, check with your instructor or a librarian. Some libraries have periodicals (magazines, journals, and newspapers) bound in volumes; other libraries have periodicals on microfilm, or microfiche, or in unbound stacks. Once you discover which format your library provides, you can begin locating specific articles to read.

Usually, people read magazines for opinions and evaluations of topics rather than for current, up-to-the-moment news. Certain magazines written by scholars or specialists in a particular field are called *journals*. These publications are usually the most accurate, authoritative sources available for research. There are literally hundreds of magazines and journals available, ranging from news and business publications to special-interest publications.

■ A Student Writes

After several class discussions on writing the research-based essay and the benefits of using other people's ideas for support in an essay, Maggie's instructor gave the class a new assignment: to take their essays on censorship (described in Part One) and add at least two outside sources for support. The instructor explained that the purpose of this assignment was to show that the ideas of others can be used to illustrate, expand, or give examples of major points made in the censorship essays.

To begin the research process, Maggie decided to reexamine her essay to look for key words that would help her locate information. She reread each paragraph in her draft carefully and came up with a focused list of key words.

21d

KEY WORDS

    censorship
    freedom of the press
    government and the press
    freedom of speech
    security classification (government documents)

Next, Maggie asked Larry if he would read her draft and offer some suggestions for key words.

◪ A Classmate Responds

QUESTION FOR REVIEW

Are there words stated or implied in the essay that might be used as key words? Which ones?

Larry gave Maggie several suggestions.

LARRY'S RESPONSES

newspapers — censorship
official secrets
television broadcasting — censorship

Maggie then checked the *Library of Congress Subject Headings* to see if these terms were used as headings in indexes. She wanted to be sure that these terms would help her locate information specific enough to support the ideas in her essay. Her next step was to use the key terms to find sources listed in periodical indexes. Her work on this next step is explained at the end of chapter 22.

Chapter 22

Taking Notes

22a Finding the Right Sources

There are usually many books, articles, and essays on any particular topic. When faced with several shelves of books or a page with 10 or more articles listed on the topic, how do you choose the best ones? If you choose a book, look for your key words in the table of contents and in the index. When you find one of your key words in the table of contents or in the index, briefly check the pages listed to see whether you can use the information. Once you learn to use books in this manner, you can look through a book quickly to determine if it can be useful. This method is fast and effective.

A similar method is useful when searching for magazine or journal articles. Look carefully at the titles of the articles listed in the index to see whether any of your key words are included. If a summary of the article is provided, check it to decide whether the article seems relevant. If a key word is not listed and no summary is provided, you will simply have to look up the article. Then skim the article to see whether any of your key words are present. If a key word is mentioned and the article contains specific information related to your ideas about the topic, read the article carefully and take notes. If your key words are not mentioned, skim just a few sentences in each paragraph of the article to determine whether the writer presents ideas that you can use as support in your writing or ideas that provide a basis for argument.

Note that if you sit down, read an article, and take notes immediately, you may discover midway through the article that the ideas presented are biased, distorted, untrue, or unrelated to the focus of your paper. Thus, you will have wasted valuable time taking notes. If you skim the article first, you can quickly reject any article not relevant to your topic.

22b Reading the Sources

When reading books and articles on your topic, keep in mind what you know about bias and distortion of information (see section 1a-9). If you have read several different sources and notice that a particular person is referred to repeatedly, you may want to research that person to determine the significance he or she has to your topic. Likewise, if key ideas or specific information are repeated in several sources, the information is probably reliable. If, on the other hand, similar information appears in several sources and obvious contradictions or discrepancies appear in another source, the contradictions and discrepancies probably illustrate either an opposing view or a bias or distortion of information.

Also, be aware that publications of special-interest groups usually have a definite bias. For example, a publication of the People for the Ethical Treatment of Animals (PETA) will examine the exploitation of animals in drug research and not mention the marketable results, whereas a publication like *FDA Consumer* will examine the advances in marketing drugs and not mention the possible exploitation of animals used in the drug research.

After you find sources you can use, and after a preliminary reading of them, you can begin to take notes. There are several productive ways to note important information from these sources. You can highlight, underline, or make marginal notations on a photocopy of the chapter or article. You can also take notes on a separate piece of paper, although this method can become confusing if you forget to properly document the information. A productive, well-organized method for taking notes is to put ideas on note cards.

22b

22c Making Note Cards

A **note card** lists one idea, fact, paraphrase, quotation, or summary from a source. When you read an article (or chapter, or book) and take notes on note cards, use the same-size cards — 3 × 5– or 4 × 6–inch index cards — and indicate whether the information is a quotation, a paraphrase, a summary, your own idea, or a conclusion you reached while reading. Also indicate the page number of the source of the information on each card.

You can experiment to find the method that works best for you. You may want to put the author, title, and page number of the work on each card; or you may note just the author's name and page number. Or you might use a numerical or alphabetical system: All cards labeled 1 are from source 1, all cards labeled 2 are from source 2, and so on; or all cards labeled A are from source A, and so forth. If you use a numerical or alphabetical system, be sure to indicate at least the page number of the source on the note card itself.

The following sample note cards were compiled for a paper on animal rights. The writer has used the author–page number method and has labeled the cards according to the type of note.

As mentioned previously, you have several options for taking notes. You can use your note cards to list quotations, to note quotations you will change into paraphrases later, to paraphrase

Sample Note Cards

22c

Cattle "are treated as industrial products from birth to slaughter."

Rifkin p. 287

[quotation]

> *Mass-produced chickens are not really farm animals. Instead of living in a barnyard, they live in cages in factorylike buildings that have no natural light. Real barnyards are practically nonexistent. Instead, there are factories that use an assembly line production that does not include compassion for chickens as living beings.*
>
> Robbins p. 53
>
> [paraphrase]

> *chickens — debeaked to prevent pecking*
>   *claws grow to wire cages*
>   *filthy cages*
>   *unsanitary conditions*
>   *hung on conveyor belt*
>
> Singer pp. 96-102
>
> [summary of ideas]

ideas, and to note questions or ideas that occur to you as you read. Once you have your notes on cards, you can organize them by author or by similar ideas and begin to consider their use in your essay.

22d

22d Quoting

A **quotation** is any word or words taken directly from a source. You can indicate quotations in one of two ways. To indicate a short quotation, use quotation marks before and after the quoted words.

John Robbins, in his book *Diet for a New America*, says, "I see us realizing that all God's critters have a place in the choir" (47).

Indicate a long quotation by indenting it from the rest of the text (see section 23b-2). Use long quotations when you need an expert's opinion to make your argument more credible, when you cannot paraphrase information accurately, when you find a statement that is clear and useful that you do not want to paraphrase, and when you find a statement that you simply cannot state in a better way.

22e Paraphrasing

Paraphrasing means taking someone's ideas and putting them into your own words. Paraphrasing does not mean changing only the order of words in a sentence or changing only the verb tenses. Usually, a paraphrase contains roughly the same number of words as the original, as in the following example.

ORIGINAL

A DIET FOR A NEW AMERICA

To begin with, today's chicken farms are not really "farms" anymore, but should more accurately be called "chicken factories." Factories, because the chickens live their whole lives inside buildings entirely devoid of natural light. The day of the barnyard is long gone. There are no barns and no yards in today's mechanized world of poultry production, only assembly lines, conveyer belts, and fluorescent lights. Factories, because these proud and sensitive creatures are treated strictly as merchandise, with utter contempt for their spirits, with not a trace of feeling or compassion for the fact that they are living, breathing animals. Factories, because the chickens are systematically deprived of every conceivable expression of their natural urges.

ACCEPTABLE PARAPHRASE

Mass-produced chickens are not really farm animals as much as they are factory animals. Instead of living in a barnyard, they live in cages in factorylike buildings that have no natural light. Real barnyards are nonexistent. Instead, factories use an assem-

22e

bly line production that does not include compassion for chickens as living beings. Chickens are deprived of their sensitivity and pride and are treated not as animals with instincts but as merchandise (Robbins 53).

The paraphrased example uses the main idea from the original without changing the meaning of the original statement, and it illustrates the necessary documentation. Use paraphrasing to provide a smooth and cohesive way to incorporate someone else's ideas into your writing.

22f   Summarizing

A **summary** is a brief restatement of the main ideas in a source or a section of a source. Generally, a summary is much shorter than the original. For example, a summary of a long paragraph might be a single sentence. A summary does not include specific details, and it does not include your opinion of the author's ideas. Once you write the summary and note the source of the ideas, you can state your opinion of how the information supports or contradicts your own ideas.

Here is an acceptable summary of the paragraph from *Diet for a New America* in Section 22e.

22f

ACCEPTABLE SUMMARY

Chickens are no longer treated as living beings but as consumable goods by those who raise them for food (Robbins 53).

Notice that the summary is stated in the writer's own words yet conveys the full meaning of the original paragraph. It indicates that the way chickens raised for food today are treated is worse than the way they were treated in the past. It also shows that the author of the source doesn't think that the present treatment is acceptable by contrasting the words *living beings* with *consumable goods*.

22g Avoiding Plagiarism

Plagiarism means to use someone else's ideas or examples (whether or not you change the wording) without giving appropriate credit to that person. Be careful to credit (document) all summaries, paraphrases, and quotations that you use to support your own ideas. Make sure that summaries and paraphrases are your words rather than a rearrangement of an author's words, and always check quotations for accurate wording.

Compare the following original sentence and the plagiarized sentence.

ORIGINAL

> To begin with, today's chicken farms are not really "farms" anymore, but should more accurately be called "chicken factories."
>
> —John Robbins, *Diet for a New America* (p. 53)

PLAGIARIZED PARAPHRASE

> First of all, today's chicken farms aren't farms, but should be called chicken factories (Robbins 53).

This paraphrase is not acceptable because the writer has not restated the author's ideas; instead, the writer has merely omitted a few words. Unless quotation marks are used, the writer implies that the words are his or hers rather than the original author's.

The next two examples demonstrate an acceptable paraphrase and an acceptable way to use a quotation.

22g

ACCEPTABLE PARAPHRASE

> Mass-produced chickens are not really farm animals as much as they are factory animals (Robbins 53).

ACCEPTABLE QUOTATION

> Robbins thinks "chicken factories" is a more accurate choice of words than "chicken farms" to describe the conditions of chickens raised for food today (53).

22h Keeping Bibliography Cards

A **bibliography card** lists all the publication information of one source. A bibliography card for a book lists the author, title, city of publication, publishing company, and year of publication. A bibliography card for a magazine or newspaper article lists the author (if given), title of article, title of magazine or newspaper, date, and page numbers of the article. Bibliography cards are useful when you are writing a research-based essay because they make organizing your list of sources easy. They help you to alphabetize and correctly indicate your list of sources.

One effective way to make bibliography cards is to use the same-size cards (3 × 5– or 4 × 6–inch index cards) for all of your sources. While you are doing your research, list one source on each card. For example, if you have found five different articles on advertising, put the bibliographic information for each article on a separate index card. When you write information on the cards, make sure that you use the correct Modern Language Association (MLA) or other documentation format (see the sample bibliography cards that follow). Then when you prepare the Works Cited or Bibliography page, all the correct information in the appropriate order will be right in front of you. Once the

Sample Bibliography Cards

22h

MLA Style

Rifkin, Jeremy. *Beyond Beef: The Rise and Fall of the Cattle Culture*. New York: Dutton, 1992.

> Robbins, John. _Diet for a New America_.
> Walpole, NH: Stillpoint, 1987.

> Singer, Peter. _Animal Liberation_. New York:
> Avon, 1977.

information is on cards, you will be able to alphabetize and copy them.

22h

■ A Student Writes

For an exercise in developing skills crucial to writing a research-based essay, Maggie's instructor asked the class to find and summarize a short article on censorship in a current magazine. The purpose of this assignment was to find some information that might be used as support in the censorship essay and to practice summarizing other people's ideas. Maggie used a short article from *Time*.

ORIGINAL

ABORTION ABOUT-FACE

Clinton's First Big Batch of Orders Lifts a Number of Reagan-Bush Prohibitions

Even before he had time to feel settled in the Oval Office, Bill Clinton began a sweeping reversal of 12 years of Republican policy. The President on Friday signed several major White House orders. One abolished Dan Quayle's Council on Competitiveness, which critics had assailed for weakening environmental regulations. The others all concerned abortion. Clinton ended the Reagan-Bush "gag rule" on abortion counseling at federally financed clinics and lifted prohibitions on fetal-tissue research, abortion at military hospitals and funding for overseas population-control programs. Said Clinton: "We must free science and medicine from the grasp of politics." No way. Protesters who had gathered at the White House to decry the Supreme Court's *Roe v. Wade* decision of 20 years ago (the coincidence of the anniversary and the orders was no coincidence whatever) blamed Clinton's "wicked counselors" and vowed to fight on.

— *Time,* 1 Feb. 1993: 17

Maggie used paraphrase and quotation in her summary in order to present the author's main ideas as clearly as possible. She was careful not to include her own opinion at this point because her purpose was to restate the author's ideas.

MAGGIE'S SUMMARY

On Friday, 29 January 1993, President Bill Clinton changed "12 years of Republican policy" ("Abortion" 17). He eliminated former Vice President Quayle's Counsel on Competitiveness, which had been criticized for making environmental regulations weak. He also eliminated the abortion-counseling gag rule placed on federally funded clinics and the bans on "fetal-tissue research," performing abortions at military hospitals, and federal "funding for overseas population-control programs" (17).

Maggie asked Miguel to read her summary and answer the questions on the instructor's handout.

☑ A Classmate Responds

QUESTIONS FOR REVIEW

1. Does the summary use a combination of paraphrase and quotation?
2. Are the quotations clearly introduced and incorporated into the sentences?
3. Are the quotations documented?
4. Is the summary free of the writer's opinion?

Miguel's answers were brief.

MIGUEL'S RESPONSES

1. There are a few quotations but not too many.
2. Yes; none of the sentences begins with a quotation.
3. Yes.
4. Yes.

Maggie was pleased with Miguel's comments and was ready to go on to the next step in her research.

■ A Student Writes

Maggie was ready to use her key terms to find information in *Readers' Guide*. She came across the following entries.

READERS' GUIDE ENTRIES

Freedom of speech
> *See also*
> Freedom of the press
> Libel and slander
> Farrakhan and Sakharov. M. Stone. il *U S News World Rep*
> 97:72 Ag 20 '84

Freedom of the press
> *See also*
> Government and the press
> Libel and slander
> First Amendment junkies. *New Repub* 191:6 Ag 6 '84

She then located and read these articles, but she was not sure if the information was too dated to be of use in her essay. She decided to ask Miguel for more feedback. He read through her note cards and answered the questions on the handout.

☑ A Classmate Responds

QUESTIONS FOR REVIEW

1. How recent is the information?
2. Is it possible that there is more recent research?

Miguel's answers were direct and very helpful.

MIGUEL'S RESPONSES

1. These articles are from 1984 and are not really recent enough to give current information on the topic.
2. Definitely. There probably have been many recent court cases on the topic.

■ A Student Writes

Maggie appreciated Miguel's responses and decided not to use the information in the articles. She knew she could use information from the article she had summarized for her instructor, and she found a copy of the First Amendment in a political science textbook. She also decided to spend some time discussing censorship with one of her classmates who is a Vietnamese student. She then took notes from these sources and wrote those notes on cards. (See the sample note cards that follow.)

Once she had finished the note cards, Maggie wrote bibliography cards that included all the information she would need for her Works Cited page. (See the sample bibliography cards that follow.)

Maggie incorporated the information from her note cards into her original draft, and she used the information from her bibliography cards to structure the Works Cited page at the end of her essay. The revised draft with the Works Cited page added is reprinted at the end of chapter 23.

Sample Note Cards

The First Amendment says, "Congress shall make no law . . . abridging the freedom of speech or of the press."

Burns and Peltason p. 764

[quotation]

The Reagan-Bush administration implemented a "gag rule" on federally funded clinics. This rule stipulated that abortion counseling was prohibited at these particular clinics.

"Abortion" p. 17

[paraphrase]

Vietnam — different laws
    government *is* media
    media controlled by government
    media is progovernment
    little truth is published or broadcast

Su interview

[summary of ideas]

Sample Bibliography Cards

"Abortion About-Face". <u>Time</u> 1 Feb. 1993: 17.

Burns, James M., and Jack W. Peltason.
    <u>Government by the People: The Dynamics</u>
    <u>of American National Governmnent.</u>
    6th ed. Englewood Cliffs: Prentice, 1966.

Su, Hoang V. Personal interview.
    18 Nov. 1992.

Chapter 23

Drafting the Research-Based Essay

23a Using Note Cards

Once you have done your research, you have several ways to use the information you have found. One way is to organize all the note cards according to specific categories (key words, similar ideas, and the like) and take each stack of related note cards and write a paragraph or more for the stack. Then you can organize the paragraphs according to your preliminary outline. A second way to use the information is to write a draft from memory (without looking at your notes) and then use the note cards to help you locate ideas that need to be documented. A third way to use the information is as support for a draft you have written either before or after your preliminary reading on the topic.

The focus of a research-based essay should be on your ideas as a writer, what you have to say about a topic or an issue, and whether or not you can argue and show support for your ideas. Having a rough draft in hand while doing research gives you some sense of which ideas you want or need to emphasize, which ideas need explanations or examples, and which ideas need support from experts. Having a rough draft before doing research also helps you to set reasonable boundaries for your search. Your ideas and not the ideas from other sources should dominate and control your essay.

23a

23b Integrating and Documenting Sources

23b-1 Introduce Short Quotations

When using quotations in an essay, you need to give the reader some indication of the significance of the quotation or its connection to your ideas. Most readers expect quotations to be integrated into your work in a certain way — with an introduction that is smooth and clear followed with a comment on the importance or relevance of the quotation to the point you are making. This integration helps make the written text more cohesive. Although it isn't incorrect to place appropriate quotations between your sentences (a glued-together structure), it usually isn't the most effective way to write. Look at this example.

> John Robbins, in his book *Diet for a New America*, says a lot about animals. "I see us realizing that all God's critters have a place in the choir" (47).

This is not a smooth presentation of the quotation. A better introduction presents the quotation as a part of the writer's own sentence.

> John Robbins, in his book *Diet for a New America*, says, "I see us realizing that all God's critters have a place in the choir" (47).

23b

Try to use a variety of introductions for the quotations you cite.

> *According to* Peter Singer, ". . ." (32).
>
> John Robbins *explains that* ". . ." (45).
>
> Animal rights activists *agree on* ". . ." (Jones 87).
>
> As one noted researcher *has mentioned*, ". . ." (Smith 775).

23b-2 Introduce Long Quotations

In general, use long quotations (four lines or longer, as suggested by the MLA) sparingly, only when you need to restate for the sake of clarity or argument lines of dialogue, poetry, or other written forms. Most long quotations are introduced with an independent clause (a complete sentence) and a colon. The following example illustrates an acceptable format.

EXAMPLE

Quotation is introduced

> In his book about animal rights, John Robbins explains how chicken farms today are quite different from farms of past years:

MLA style: entire quotation indented 10 spaces from left margin

> To begin with, today's chicken farms are not really "farms" anymore, but should more accurately be called "chicken factories." Factories, because the chickens live their whole lives inside buildings entirely devoid of natural light. The day of the barnyard is long gone. There are no barns and no yards in today's mechanized world of poultry production, only assembly lines, conveyer belts, and fluorescent lights. (Robbins 53)

Writer's comment about quotation

> Few people are aware of the living conditions of these animals and the cruelty and suffering they endure for the convenience of the factory owners. Some people forget that animals are living beings with a place in the order of the world.

23b

After quoting a source, provide a follow-up comment to reinforce the significance or importance of the quotation. Ask yourself why you chose this particular quotation and what it means to you. When you introduce quotations and give follow-up comments on them, you add the connections needed to make your research writing cohesive.

23b-3 Use MLA In-Text Citations

Any time you use someone else's ideas, even if you put these ideas into your own words, you need to indicate where you got the information. The way you indicate this information — that is, the style of documentation you use — depends on the demands of the particular discipline you are writing for. In English courses and in most of the humanities (fine arts, theater arts, speech and communication, modern or classical languages, literature, music, religion), use MLA documentation. The MLA form of documentation is parenthetical — that is, sources are indicated in parentheses at the end of a sentence. This method is a relatively simple one for citing information. Generally, the parentheses include an author's last name, a page reference, and possibly an abbreviated form of the title of the author's work if you use more than one work by the same author. The reader can find complete bibliographic information on the Works Cited page at the end of the paper. The following examples illustrate in-text documentation.

QUOTATION

The child's mother understood that "yesterday was only the beginning" (Brown 32). [Brown is the author, and 32 is the page where the quotation appears in Brown's work.]

One member of Congress mentioned that "someone will have to accept responsibility for raising taxes" ("Taxes" 16). [This article, "Taxes," does not list an author. Therefore, an abbreviated form of the title is used for the reference.]

PARAPHRASE

While there are people to fight tyranny, dictators will continue to lose power (Schlenk 47). [Notice that a paraphrase citation includes a page reference.]

Very few people agreed that taxes should be raised ("Taxes" 16).

Notice in all of the examples that the parentheses are actually a part of the sentence, and, therefore, the period goes *after* the parentheses.

23b

23c Moving from Discovery Draft to the Essay

Let's say that after some preliminary reading, you have written the following discovery draft.

DISCOVERY DRAFT

Animal rights is an issue that fascinates me and frightens me. It fascinates me because there are so many different groups of people that want everyone to know what happens to animals raised for food. These groups say we should boycott certain meat like beef because of the inhumane ways the cows are treated.

I get frightened when I think about the ways animals are used to test drugs and chemicals used in cosmetics. When the animals are used in lab experiments, they are treated cruelly and are tortured. For example, rabbits are used to test chemicals used in eye makeup. Chemicals are put into the rabbits' eyes, which are then taped shut. If the chemicals don't harm the rabbits' eyes, they are considered to be safe to put in the makeup for humans.

What can people do to stop this cruelty? Will it really matter if we simply stop eating a certain kind of meat or stop buying a particular brand of makeup? Some products even carry labels that say no animals were used to test the product.

After you have written the discovery draft, used key words from your preliminary research or a brainstorming list to find books and articles on animal rights, read the books and articles, written note cards (organized by related ideas), you will need to integrate some of these new ideas into your draft. How do you revise your draft?

First, look at the draft to see whether you can add more of your own ideas to strengthen or further develop it. With a few changes — reworking paragraph 1 to include more background information, clarifying the thesis, writing another body paragraph, deleting the last sentence, adding information to the conclusion — the draft becomes more cohesive.

23c

REVISED DRAFT

Animal rights is currently an issue that is causing profound reactions in people. Years ago, few people thought twice about eating chicken or veal, wearing fur coats, using leather products, or using cosmetics. Today, however, with the massive food, clothing, and cosmetic industries looking for ways to cut costs and increase profits, the rights of animals have been overlooked. Activist groups like People for the Ethical Treatment of Animals (PETA) want the public to know how animals raised for consumption and animals used in lab settings are treated.

Groups like PETA and the Fund for Animals say we should boycott meat like chicken and beef because of the inhumane ways the animals are raised and processed for meat. [need examples]

When animals are used to test chemicals in cosmetics, they are tortured and treated cruelly. For example, rabbits are used to test chemicals used in eye makeup. Chemicals are put into the rabbits' eyes, which are then taped shut. [test name?] If the chemicals do not harm the rabbits' eyes, they are considered to be safe for use in makeup for humans.

What can people do to stop this cruelty? If enough consumers refuse to buy certain types of meat or refuse to buy certain products like cosmetics that use animals for research, will the boycott result in the elimination of animal cruelty in food production and in product testing? If not, it will at least send a message to the industries that some consumers are taking a stand for animal rights, and it will help some people sleep better at night knowing that they may have saved at least one animal.

Notice in the draft the bracketed suggestions for adding ideas. These places need examples for support.

23c

The next step is to examine your note cards, find information that is related to the ideas in your draft, locate a logical and appropriate place for them, and integrate them into the text. In order to integrate new ideas, you may have to rephrase, add, or delete some of your original information, or you may simply have to introduce and comment on the quotations, paraphrases, or summaries you plan to add.

The completed draft (new information is integrated, but the draft is not yet revised or edited) follows.

Next, you need to check the quotations, paraphrases, and summaries you have used.

1. Are the quotations accurate?
2. Are they clearly introduced and commented on?
3. Are the paraphrases accurate?

Completed Draft [not proofread or edited]

Animal rights is currently an issue that is causing profound reactions in people. Years ago, few people thought twice about eating chicken or beef, wearing fur coats, using leather products, or using cosmetics. Today, with the massive food, clothing, and cosmetic industries looking for ways to meet production demands, cut costs, and increase profits, the rights of animals have been overlooked and often ignored. Activist groups like People for the Ethical Treatment of Animals want the public to know how animals raised for consumption and animals used in lab settings are treated.

Groups like PETA and the Fund for Animals say we should boycott meat like chicken because of the inhumane ways the animals are raised and processed. Few people know what really happens to chickens from the day they hatch. Rarely do the chickens' feet touch the ground — they go directly from the incubator to a cage that contains so many of them that they can barely move. They are usually debeaked to prevent pecking, which might damage the animal and reduce profits; and as they grow, their claws sometimes grow to the wire flooring of the cages (Singer 138). The cages are not cleaned, which results in extremely unsanitary conditions. When the chickens have grown sufficiently, they are hung by their feet on a conveyer belt and slaughtered (Singer 96–102).

1
Paraphrase of information from Singer

2
Summary of information from Singer

3
A whole
paragraph of
information
added from
Robbins

Mass-produced chickens are not really farm animals

3

as much as they are factory animals. Instead of living in a

barnyard, they live in cages in factorylike buildings that

have no natural light. Real barnyards are practically

nonexistent. Instead, there are factories that use an

assembly line production that does not include compassion

for chickens as living beings. These creatures are deprived of

their sensitivity and pride and are treated not as animals

with instincts but as merchandise (Robbins 53).

Animal rights activists say we should also boycott beef

because of the inhumane treatment of cattle, which are not

4
A brief
quotation
strengthens
the
argument

treated as animals but "as industrial products from birth to

4

slaughter" (Rifkin 287). Most cattle are raised in crowded,

unsanitary conditions, fed hormones and steroids to quicken

their growth, shipped long distances in poorly ventilated

trucks, herded through slaughter lines, and killed in what

often is a long, agonizing process (Singer 142–155; Robbins

103–108). This creature bears little resemblance to the

ground beef consumers buy at grocery stores. In fact, most

people would not be able to even think about eating this meat

if they knew what these animals endured.

Another area of concern is the use of animals in

research, particularly in the cosmetics industry. When

animals are used to test chemicals in cosmetics, they are

tortured and treated cruelly. For example, rabbits are used to test chemicals used in eye makeup. Chemicals are put into the rabbits' eyes, which are then taped shut. This procedure

5 is the Draize test, a standard method used by the US Food and Drug Administration (Singer 48). If the chemicals do not harm the rabbits' eyes, they are considered safe for use in makeup for humans.

5

The precise name of the test added

What can people do to stop this cruelty? If enough consumers refuse to buy certain types of meat or refuse to buy certain types of cosmetics, will the boycott result in the elimination of animal cruelty in food production and product testing and restore the rights to animals? If not, it will at least send a message to the industries that some consumers are taking a stand for animal rights, and it will help some people sleep better at night knowing that they may have saved at least one animal.

4. Are they placed appropriately?
5. Are the summaries accurate?
6. Are they placed appropriately?
7. Is everything documented correctly?

Once you determine that the information you have gathered is accurate and is placed correctly and appropriately in your draft, you can revise, proofread, and edit the draft. Finally, you will need to organize the Works Cited page.

23d Works Cited Page

At the end of the paper, the page listing all the sources referred to within the paper is called the **Works Cited** page. This list is alphabetized by authors' last names; or if no author is listed in the work, it is alphabetized by the first major word in the title of the article (but not *a, an,* or *the*). The Works Cited page always starts a new page with the centered heading "Works Cited" and belongs after the last page of the essay. The following examples illustrate some of the ways to list sources. (For types of sources not listed, refer to Joseph Gibaldi and Walter S. Achtert, eds., *The MLA Handbook for Writers of Research Papers*, 3rd ed., New York: MLA, 1988.)

23d

BOOKS

Author's last name, first name. *Title of Book*. City of publication: name of publishing company, year.

EXAMPLE

Comprone, Joseph. *From Experience to Expression*. Boston: Houghton, 1981.

MAGAZINE ARTICLES

Author's last name, first name. "Title of Article." *Name of Magazine* day month year: page numbers.

EXAMPLE

> Kinsley, Michael. "Visiting a Place Called Hope." *Time* 19
> Apr. 1993: 74.

NEWSPAPER ARTICLE

> Author's last name, first name. "Title of Article." *Name of
> Newspaper* day month year, edition: page numbers.

EXAMPLE

> Willis, Cary B. "Living? Or Just Existing?" *The Courier-
> Journal* 27 June 1992, metro ed.: A1, A4.

Notice that the second line of each entry is indented five spaces from the left margin.

If no author is listed for a magazine or newspaper article, begin the entry with the title.

EXAMPLE

> "Scalpel! Laser! Retrovirus!" *Time* 22 June 1992: 30–35.

INTERVIEWS

> Person's last name, first name. Personal interview. Day
> month year.

EXAMPLE

> McAdam, Rita. Personal interview. 16 Nov. 1992.

The Works Cited page for the essay on animal rights should have the following entries.

23d

Works Cited

Rifkin, Jeremy. *Beyond Beef: The Rise and Fall of the Cattle
Culture*. New York: Dutton, 1992.
Robbins, John. *Diet for a New America*. Walpole, NH: Still-
point, 1987.
Singer, Peter. *Animal Liberation*. New York: Avon, 1977.

Once the entries are alphabetized, typed on a separate page that is the last page of the essay, the finished essay should look like the essay reproduced in the following section.

23e Sample Essay

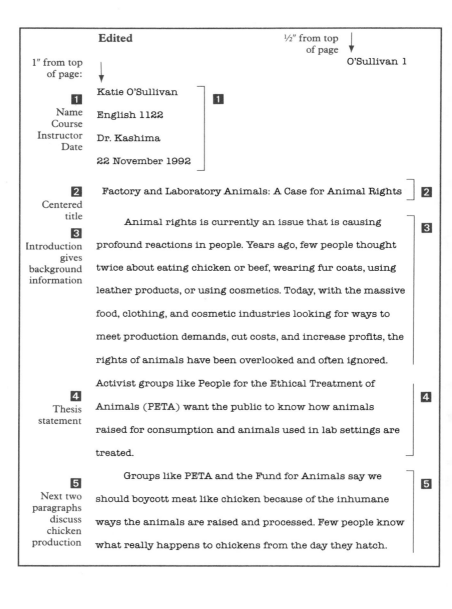

Edited

½" from top
of page

O'Sullivan 1

1" from top
of page:

1
Name
Course
Instructor
Date

Katie O'Sullivan

1

English 1122

Dr. Kashima

22 November 1992

2
Centered
title

Factory and Laboratory Animals: A Case for Animal Rights

2

3
Introduction
gives
background
information

Animal rights is currently an issue that is causing

3

profound reactions in people. Years ago, few people thought

twice about eating chicken or beef, wearing fur coats, using

leather products, or using cosmetics. Today, with the massive

food, clothing, and cosmetic industries looking for ways to

meet production demands, cut costs, and increase profits, the

rights of animals have been overlooked and often ignored.

Activist groups like People for the Ethical Treatment of

4
Thesis
statement

Animals (PETA) want the public to know how animals

4

raised for consumption and animals used in lab settings are

treated.

5
Next two
paragraphs
discuss
chicken
production

Groups like PETA and the Fund for Animals say we

5

should boycott meat like chicken because of the inhumane

ways the animals are raised and processed. Few people know

what really happens to chickens from the day they hatch.

O'Sullivan 2

5 Rarely do the chickens' feet touch the ground—they go directly from the incubator to a cage that contains so many of them that they can barely move. They are usually debeaked to prevent pecking, which might damage the animal and reduce profits; and as they grow, their claws sometimes grow **6** to the wire flooring of the cages (Singer 138). The cages are not cleaned, which results in extremely unsanitary conditions. When the chickens have grown sufficiently, they are hung by their feet on a conveyer belt and slaughtered **7** (Singer 96–102).

Mass-produced chickens are not really farm animals as much as they are factory animals. Instead of living in a barnyard, they live in cages in factorylike buildings that have no natural light. Real barnyards are practically nonexistent. Instead, there are factories that use an assembly line production that does not include compassion for chickens as living beings. These creatures are deprived of their sensitivity and pride and are treated not as animals with instincts but as merchandise (Robbins 53).

8 Animal rights activists say we should also boycott beef because of the inhumane treatment of cattle, which are not **9** treated as animals but "as industrial products from birth to slaughter" (Rifkin 287). Most cattle are raised in crowded, unsanitary conditions, fed hormones and steroids to quicken their growth, shipped long distances in poorly ventilated

---

Sidebar annotations:

Last name and page number at top right margin of each page (½″ from top of page)

6 Author and page number in parentheses

7 Cites all the pages from which summary is taken

8 Next paragraph focuses on beef

9 Quotation integrated into writer's own sentence

O'Sullivan 3

8
continued

trucks, herded through slaughter lines, and killed in what

often is a long, agonizing process (Singer 142–155; Robbins

103–108). This creature bears little resemblance to the

ground beef consumers buy at grocery stores. In fact, most

people would not be able to even think about eating this meat

if they knew what these animals endured.

10
The last
body
paragraph
discusses
animals in
lab settings

Another area of concern is the use of animals in

research, particularly in the cosmetics industry. When

animals are used to test chemicals in cosmetics, they are

tortured and treated cruelly. For example, rabbits are used to

test chemicals in eye makeup. Chemicals are put into the

rabbits' eyes, which are then taped shut. This procedure is

the Draize test, a standard method used by the US Food and

Drug Administration (Singer 48). If the chemicals do not

harm the rabbits' eyes, they are considered safe for use in

makeup for humans.

11
Conclusion's
call to action
asks readers
to respond to
inhumane
treatment of
animals

What can people do to stop this cruelty? If enough

consumers refuse to buy certain types of meat or refuse to

buy certain types of cosmetics, will the boycott result in the

elimination of animal cruelty in food production and product

testing and restore the rights to animals? If not, it will at

least send a message to the industries that some consumers

are taking a stand for animal rights, and it will help some

people sleep better at night knowing that they may have

saved at least one animal.

Works Cited
is on a
separate
page

12 | Works Cited

12
Title is
centered

13

Rifkin, Jeremy. <u>Beyond Beef: The Rise and Fall of the Cattle</u>

    <u>Culture</u>. New York: Dutton, 1992.

Robbins, John. <u>Diet for a New America</u>. Walpole, NH: Stillpoint,

    1987.

Singer, Peter. <u>Animal Liberation</u>. New York: Avon, 1977.

13
Entries are
alphabetical

14

14
State is given
if city is not
well known

Entries are
double-
spaced

23f Other Forms of Documentation

Researchers in the social sciences (psychology, sociology, history, political science, education, geography, anthropology, economics) use the American Psychological Association (APA) documentation, known as the author-date method. For information on this type of documentation, refer to the *Publication Manual of the American Psychological Association* (3rd ed.), published by the American Psychological Association.

Other documentation manuals exist for natural science and health science writing. These manuals provide complete information about the styles of documentation used in specific disciplines and are usually available in the reference section of the library. Check with your instructor to find out which manual best suits your needs for a particular course.

■ A Student Writes

23f

With her new information on cards, Maggie was ready to look for logical places in the draft to add the information. As she reread each of her paragraphs, she asked herself several questions: (1) For example? (2) What does someone else say about this? (3) Can I expand on this? Asking these questions helped her to locate ideas in her draft that could use further support. She then used some of the information word for word from her note cards and rephrased other notes as she added the new information. She carefully documented these new ideas to make it clear to her readers where the information originated.

REVISED DRAFT WITH RESEARCH ADDED

Why Does the US Government Censor Information?

US government censorship of information involves censoring official secrets that ensure national security, which includes limiting the public's right to know about foreign and domestic policies. In a democracy people usually have a right to know what their government is doing in domestic as well as foreign affairs. Sometimes, however, the government needs to ensure that certain information does not fall into the wrong hands. Differentiating between government censorship of information and government control of the news media helps to clarify the distinction between what people need to know and what they have a right to know. Government censorship of information is the deliberate withholding of information for specific reasons (usually national security), whereas government control of the news media is dictating to the media what it will and will not broadcast or print. However, in some Asian and European countries, where people's rights are different from those in the states, the government controls the news media and severely limits what can be broadcast or printed to protect leaders and to suppress truth. For example, the government in Vietnam decides what the media transmits, and the information is usually progovernment, with little or no regard for the truth (Su). The American government, however, often censors information for national security reasons and not necessarily to infringe upon the public's right to know.

Sometimes, the American government censors information to protect national security. Since television and radio news is broadcast worldwide, people in the states as well as people overseas get up-to-the-minute reports on events, reports that used to take hours, even days, to receive. If everyone around the world has the opportunity to receive such reports, information the American government does not want known internationally, or even nationally, often is withheld — censored. For example, during the Desert Storm situation information vital to the American effort was withheld from people in the states as well as people elsewhere. Strategies crucial to the military effort were classified by the government as not appropriate news.

The First Amendment to the Constitution of the United States of America lists freedom of the press as a right for citizens of this country. The amendment states the following: "Congress shall make no law . . . abridging the freedom of speech, or of the press" (Burns and Peltason 764). Freedom of the press allows certain liberties, but it is not an absolute. This freedom includes certain limitations, particularly in obtaining information. The president does have the constitutional power to withhold information deemed inappropriate or not in the interest of the people. So how does this limitation affect the citizens of this nation?

Most people are used to turning on the news on television or reading the newspaper to find out what is happening in this country and around the world. However, since the government imposes "gag rules" on the release of certain information, some information is not available to the general public. A gag rule limits or restricts discussion or release of information to the public. For example, the Reagan-Bush administration implemented a gag rule on federally funded clinics. This rule stipulated that abortion counseling was prohibited at these clinics ("Abortion" 17). The penalty for ignoring the rule was the withdrawal of federal funding. Although the media provide a public service in their dispersal of information, some government sources limit the media's access to information other than information that is in the public interest.

What about the American people's right to know what is going on in the government? People in this country have a right to know what the government is doing, but do they have a right to know every single detail? Much of what the American government does, in both domestic and foreign affairs, is a matter of public record. Only in times of war or in matters of national security does the government have a constitutional right to withhold information from the people in this country.

Obviously, there are reasons for and against the issue of government censorship of news. People need to realize that what they hear and read is limited to a certain extent and that it may not include information that the government deems inappropriate to provide. People also need to understand that this limitation is not necessarily an infringement on as much as it is an enhancement of their rights as citizens of this country.

Maggie was ready once again to ask for feedback from her classmate, Miguel. She asked him to use the list of questions provided by her instructor.

◪ A Classmate Responds

QUESTIONS FOR REVIEW

1. Does the draft seem to respond to the assignment given?
2. Can you identify the thesis?
3. What is your favorite part of the draft? What do you like about this part?
4. Which parts of the draft most effectively support the thesis? Why do you think so?
5. What is the main strength of this essay?

6. Is the introduction effective and interesting? Does it make you want to read more?
7. Are any paragraphs confusing? Which one(s)?
8. Does the researched information fit clearly and logically?
9. Are the new ideas clearly introduced?
10. Does the conclusion offer an interesting closure? Does the conclusion relate to the thesis?

Miguel's responses to the questions were short, but they showed Maggie that she had written an essay that satisfied the criteria for the assignment, discussed some aspects of censorship, and used other people's ideas for support.

MIGUEL'S RESPONSES

1. Yes, it gives other people's ideas about the topic.
2. The thesis is still the last sentence of the first paragraph.
3. I like the part about the Constitution, and I'm glad you explained about the gag rule.
4. I think all the parts support the thesis because they all tell me something about how protecting national security does not mean denying people their rights to freedom of speech.
5. The explanations are clear and the examples are ones I either know something about or want to know something about. Those are strengths because you obviously wrote with your audience in mind.
6. Yes, when you start telling the difference between what people have a right to know and what they may not need to know, I found myself wanting to know more about the topic.
7. No.
8. Yes, the quotation fits nicely, and the paraphrased information made clear what a gag rule is.
9. Yes.
10. Yes to both questions. I never thought about a limitation as a privilege before. The conclusion gave me some things to think about.

■ A Student Writes

Once she read through Miguel's comments, Maggie began to prepare the final draft. First, she transferred the information from the entries on her bibliography cards to her Works Cited page. Second, she added the proper heading to the upper left-hand corner of the first page of her paper. Third, she added page numbers and her last name to the upper right-hand corners of each page of the essay. Fourth, she proofread her draft one last time to look for and correct the following things:

> spelling errors
> typographical errors
> paragraph indenting
> documentation errors
> pagination errors

Once she had completed these steps, she was ready to submit her final copy to her instructor. This final version is reprinted on the next few pages.

Maggie MacGregor

English 1122

Dr. Besser

5 May 1993

Why Does the US Government Censor Information?

US government censorship of information involves
censoring official secrets that ensure national security,
which includes limiting the public's right to know about
foreign and domestic policies. In a democracy people usually
have a right to know what their government is doing in
domestic as well as in foreign affairs. Sometimes, however,
the government needs to ensure that certain information
does not fall into the wrong hands. Differentiating between
government censorship of information and government
control of the news media helps to clarify the distinction
between what people need to know and what they have a
right to know. Government censorship of information is the
deliberate withholding of information for specific reasons
(usually national security), whereas government control of
the news media is dictating to the media what it will and
will not broadcast or print to protect leaders and to suppress
truth. However, in some Asian and European countries,
where people's rights are different from those in the United

MacGregor 2

States, the government controls the news media and severely limits what can be broadcast or printed. For example, the government in Vietnam decides what the media transmits, and the information is usually progovernment, with little or no regard for the truth (Su). The American government, however, often censors information for national security reasons and not necessarily to infringe upon the public's right to know.

Sometimes, the American government censors information to protect national security. Since television and radio news is broadcast worldwide, people in the States as well as people overseas get up-to-the-minute reports on events, reports that used to take hours, even days, to receive. If everyone around the world has the opportunity to receive such reports, information the American government does not want known internationally, or even nationally, often is withheld — censored. For example, during the Desert Storm situation information vital to the American effort was withheld from the people in the States as well as from people elsewhere. Strategies crucial to the military effort were classified by the government as not appropriate news.

The First Amendment to the Constitution of the United States of America lists freedom of the press as a right for citizens of this country. The amendment states the following:

"Congress shall make no law . . . abridging the freedom of speech, or of the press" (Burns and Peltason 764). Freedom of the press allows certain liberties, but it is not an absolute. This freedom includes certain limitations, particularly in the obtaining of information. The president does have the constitutional power to withhold information deemed inappropriate or not in the interest of the people. So how does this affect the citizens of this nation?

Most people are used to turning on the news on television or reading the newspaper to find out what is happening in this country and around the world. However, since the government imposes "gag rules" on the release of certain information, some information is not available to the general public. A gag rule limits or restricts discussion or release of information to the public. For example, the Reagan-Bush administration implemented a gag rule on federally funded clinics. This rule stipulated that abortion counseling was prohibited at these clinics ("Abortion" 17). The penalty for ignoring the rule was the withdrawal of federal funding. Although the media provide a public service in their dispersal of information, some government sources limit the media's accessibility to information other than that which is in the public interest.

What about the American people's right to know what is going on in the government? People in this country have a

MacGregor 4

right to know what the government is doing, but do they have a right to know every single detail? Much of what the American government does, both in domestic and foreign affairs, is a matter of public record. Only in times of war or in matters of national security does the government have a constitutional right to withhold information from the people in this country.

Obviously, there are reasons for and against the issue of government censorship of news. People need to realize that what they hear and read is limited to a certain extent and that it may not include information that the government deems inappropriate to provide. People also need to understand that this limitation is not necessarily an infringement on as much as it is an enhancement of their rights as citizens of this country.

Works Cited

"Abortion About-Face." <u>Time</u> 1 Feb. 1993: 17.

Burns, James M., and Jack W. Peltason. <u>Government by the</u>
     <u>People: The Dynamics of American National</u>
     <u>Government</u>. 6th ed. Englewood Cliffs: Prentice, 1966.

Su, Hoang V. Personal interview. 18 Nov. 1992.

INDEX

Credits, *continued from the copyright page.*